Jedediah Smith
and the Mountain Men of the American West

WORLD EXPLORERS

Jedediah Smith
and the Mountain Men of the American West

John Logan Allen

Introductory Essay by Michael Collins

CHELSEA HOUSE PUBLISHERS

New York • Philadelphia

On the cover   Nineteenth-century map of the American West;
portrait of Jedediah Smith

Chelsea House Publishers
Editor-in-Chief   Remmel Nunn
Managing Editor   Karyn Gullen Browne
Copy Chief   Juliann Barbato
Picture Editor   Adrian G. Allen
Art Director   Maria Epes
Deputy Copy Chief   Mark Rifkin
Assistant Art Director   Noreen Romano
Series Design   Loraine Machlin
Manufacturing Manager   Gerald Levine
Systems Manager   Lindsey Ottman
Production Manager   Joseph Romano
Production Coordinator   Marie Claire Cebrián

World Explorers
Senior Editor   Sean Dolan

Staff for JEDEDIAH SMITH AND THE MOUNTAIN MEN OF THE AMERICAN
WEST
Associate Editor   Terrance Dolan
Copy Editor   Joseph Roman
Editorial Assistant   Martin Mooney
Picture Researcher   Vicky Haluska
Senior Designer   Basia Niemczyc

7   9   8   6

Library of Congress Cataloging-in-Publication Data

Allen, John Logan
   Jedediah Smith and the mountain men of the American West/
John Logan Allen.
      p.   cm.—(World explorers)
   Includes bibliographical references and index.
   Summary: Chronicles the exploits of the mountain men who
opened many trails and passages through the American West in the
early 19th century.
   ISBN 0-7910-1319-7
         0-7910-1543-2 (pbk.)
   1. Smith, Jedediah Strong, 1799–1831—Juvenile literature.
2. Explorers—West (U.S.)—Biography—Juvenile literature.
3. Fur traders—West (U.S.)—Biography—Juvenile literature.
4. Trappers—West (U.S.)—Biography—Juvenile literature.
5. West (U.S.)—Description and travel—To 1848—Juvenile
literature. [1. Explorers.   2. Frontier and pioneer life.   3. West
(U.S.)—Discovery and exploration.]   I. Title.   II. Series.
F592.S649A38   1991
978'.02'092—dc20   90-24825
[B]   CIP
[920]   AC

CONTENTS

WORLD EXPLORERS

THE EARLY EXPLORERS

Herodotus and the Explorers of the Classical Age
Marco Polo and the Medieval Explorers
The Viking Explorers

THE FIRST GREAT AGE OF DISCOVERY

Jacques Cartier, Samuel de Champlain, and the Explorers of Canada
Christopher Columbus and the First Voyages to the New World
From Coronado to Escalante: The Explorers of the Spanish Southwest
Hernando de Soto and the Explorers of the American South
Sir Francis Drake and the Struggle for an Ocean Empire
Vasco da Gama and the Portuguese Explorers
La Salle and the Explorers of the Mississippi
Ferdinand Magellan and the Discovery of the World Ocean
Pizarro, Orellana, and the Exploration of the Amazon
The Search for the Northwest Passage
Giovanni da Verrazano and the Explorers of the Atlantic Coast

THE SECOND GREAT AGE OF DISCOVERY

Roald Amundsen and the Quest for the South Pole
Daniel Boone and the Opening of the Ohio Country
Captain James Cook and the Explorers of the Pacific
The Explorers of Alaska
John Charles Frémont and the Great Western Reconnaissance
Alexander von Humboldt, Colossus of Exploration
Lewis and Clark and the Route to the Pacific
Alexander Mackenzie and the Explorers of Canada
Robert Peary and the Quest for the North Pole
Zebulon Pike and the Explorers of the American Southwest
John Wesley Powell and the Great Surveys of the American West
Jedediah Smith and the Mountain Men of the American West
Henry Stanley and the European Explorers of Africa
Lt. Charles Wilkes and the Great U.S. Exploring Expedition

THE THIRD GREAT AGE OF DISCOVERY

Apollo to the Moon
The Explorers of the Undersea World
The First Men in Space
The Mission to Mars and Beyond
Probing Deep Space

CHELSEA HOUSE PUBLISHERS

Into the Unknown

Michael Collins

It is difficult to define most eras in history with any precision, but not so the space age. On October 4, 1957, it burst on us with little warning when the Soviet Union launched *Sputnik*, a 184-pound cannonball that circled the globe once every 96 minutes. Less than 4 years later, the Soviets followed this first primitive satellite with the flight of Yuri Gagarin, a 27-year-old fighter pilot who became the first human to orbit the earth. The Soviet Union's success prompted President John F. Kennedy to decide that the United States should "land a man on the moon and return him safely to earth" before the end of the 1960s. We now had not only a space age but a space race.

I was born in 1930, exactly the right time to allow me to participate in Project Apollo, as the U.S. lunar program came to be known. As a young man growing up, I often found myself too young to do the things I wanted—or suddenly too old, as if someone had turned a switch at midnight. But for Apollo, 1930 was the perfect year to be born, and I was very lucky. In 1966 I enjoyed circling the earth for three days, and in 1969 I flew to the moon and laughed at the sight of the tiny earth, which I could cover with my thumbnail.

How the early explorers would have loved the view from space! With one glance Christopher Columbus could have plotted his course and reassured his crew that the world was indeed round. In 90 minutes Magellan could have looked down at every port of call in the *Victoria's* three-year circumnavigation of the globe. Given a chance to map their route from orbit, Lewis and Clark could have told President Jefferson that there was no easy Northwest Passage but that a continent of exquisite diversity awaited their scrutiny.

In a physical sense, we have already gone to most places that we can. That is not to say that there are not new adventures awaiting us deep in the sea or on the red plains of Mars, but more important than reaching new places will be understanding those we have already visited. There are vital gaps in our understanding of how our planet works as an ecosystem and how our planet fits into the infinite order of the universe. The next great age may well be the age of assimilation, in which we use microscope and telescope to evaluate what we have discovered and put that knowledge to use. The adventure of being first to reach may be replaced by the satisfaction of being first to grasp. Surely that is a form of exploration as vital to our well-being, and perhaps even survival, as the distinction of being the first to explore a specific geographical area.

The explorers whose stories are told in the books of this series did not just sail perilous seas, scale rugged mountains, traverse blistering deserts, dive to the depths of the ocean, or land on the moon. Their voyages and expeditions were journeys of mind as much as of time and distance, through which they—and all of mankind—were able to reach a greater understanding of our universe. That challenge remains, for all of us. The imperative is to see, to understand, to develop knowledge that others can use, to help nurture this planet that sustains us all. Perhaps being born in 1975 will be as lucky for a new generation of explorer as being born in 1930 was for Neil Armstrong, Buzz Aldrin, and Mike Collins.

The Reader's Journey

William H. Goetzmann

This volume is one of a series that takes us with the great explorers of the ages on bold journeys over the oceans and the continents and into outer space. As we travel along with these imaginative and courageous journeyers, we share their adventures and their knowledge. We also get a glimpse of that mysterious and inextinguishable fire that burned in the breast of men such as Magellan and Columbus—the fire that has propelled all those throughout the ages who have been driven to leave behind family and friends for a voyage into the unknown.

No one has ever satisfactorily explained the urge to explore, the drive to go to the "back of beyond." It is certain that it has been present in man almost since he began walking erect and first ventured across the African savannas. Sparks from that same fire fueled the transoceanic explorers of the Ice Age, who led their people across the vast plain that formed a land bridge between Asia and North America, and the astronauts and scientists who determined that man must reach the moon.

Besides an element of adventure, all exploration involves an element of mystery. We must not confuse exploration with discovery. Exploration is a purposeful human activity—a search for something. Discovery may be the end result of that search; it may also be an accident, as when Columbus found a whole new world while searching for the Indies. Often, the explorer may not even realize the full significance of what he has discovered, as was the case with Columbus. Exploration, on the other hand, is the product of a cultural or individual curiosity; it is a unique process that has enabled mankind to know and understand the world's oceans, continents, and polar regions. It is at the heart of scientific thinking. One of its most significant aspects is that it teaches people to ask the right questions; by doing so, it forces us to reevaluate what we think we know and understand. Thus knowledge progresses, and we are driven constantly to a new awareness and appreciation of the universe in all its infinite variety.

The motivation for exploration is not always pure. In his fascination with the new, man often forgets that others have been there before him. For example, the popular notion of the discovery of America overlooks the complex Indian civilizations that had existed there for thousands of years before the arrival of Europeans. Man's desire for conquest, riches, and fame is often linked inextricably with his quest for the unknown, but a story that touches so closely on the human essence must of necessity treat war as well as peace, avarice with generosity, both pride and humility, frailty and greatness. The story of exploration is above all a story of humanity and of man's understanding of his place in the universe.

The WORLD EXPLORERS series has been divided into four sections. The first treats the explorers of the ancient world, the Viking explorers of the 9th through the 11th centuries, and Marco Polo and the medieval explorers. The rest of the series is divided into three great ages of exploration. The first is the era of Columbus and Magellan: the period spanning the 15th and 16th centuries, which saw the discovery and exploration of the New World and the world ocean. The second might be called the age of science and imperialism, the era made possible by the scientific advances of the 17th century, which witnessed the discovery of the world's last two undiscovered continents, Australia and Antarctica, the mapping of all the continents and oceans, and the establishment of colonies all over the world. The third great age refers to the most ambitious quests of the 20th century—the probing of space and of the ocean's depths.

As we reach out into the darkness of outer space and other galaxies, we come to better understand how our ancestors confronted *oecumene,* or the vast earthly unknown. We learn once again the meaning of an unknown 18th-century sea captain's advice to navigators:

> And if by chance you make a landfall on the shores of another sea in a far country inhabited by savages and barbarians, remember you this: the greatest danger and the surest hope lies not with fires and arrows but in the quicksilver hearts of men.

At its core, exploration is a series of moral dramas. But it is these dramas, involving new lands, new people, and exotic ecosystems of staggering beauty, that make the explorers' stories not only moral tales but also some of the greatest adventure stories ever recorded. They represent the process of learning in its most expansive and vivid forms. We see that real life, past and present, transcends even the adventures of the starship *Enterprise.*

"To Ascend the River Missouri"

During the first half of the 19th century, St. Louis, a city located on the western bank of the Mississippi River just below the mouth of the Missouri River, served as the jumping-off place for all points west. St. Louis was a boomtown, but it was not gold that acted as a magnet for men seeking adventure and fortune in the West—it was "brown gold," the rich and luxuriant pelt of the beaver. An odd-looking creature with enormous, protruding front teeth, webbed hind feet, and a broad, flat tail, *Castor canadensis*, North America's largest rodent, thrived in the seemingly endless networks of rivers and streams that criss-cross the West. Prized by men and women of fashion in Europe and the eastern cities of the United States, the pelt of this improbable animal was just as important as any other economic, social, or political factor in drawing the first white men up the Missouri River, to the Rocky Mountains, and beyond. And although many of the trappers and traders who set off from St. Louis vanished into the wilderness and were never seen or heard from again, having fallen prey to any of a host of dangers (one out of every five trappers met his death on the trail), many of them did return to the city, with heaps of precious beaver pelts and, more important, with crucial information concerning the beautiful and terrible lands to the west.

Following the expedition of Lewis and Clark and the Corps of Discovery in 1804–6 a new breed of explorer, known as the mountain men, began to appear in the Rocky Mountains and the Far West. The first mountain men traveled alone and were in constant danger of attack by grizzly bears and hostile Indians.

The mountain men were drawn west for a variety of reasons, but primary among them was the beaver, which thrived along the rivers, streams, and brooks of the Rockies and the Far West. The sleek, rich pelt of the beaver drew a high price on the open market.

Like any boomtown, St. Louis was a colorful, raucous, and often cruel place, frequented by a wide variety of characters. Newly rich beaver barons, impeccably dressed in the latest European fashions, supervised the construction of opulent mansions by day and escorted fine ladies to balls and to the theater in the evening. On the waterfront, drifters, prostitutes, gamblers, rivermen, Indians, miners, wagoners, thugs, rogues, outlaws, and adventurers of all sorts streamed in and out of the plentiful bars, taverns, hotels, and brothels. In the muddy streets, horses and mules sank up to their knees and wagons sank up to their axles. Drunkenness was rampant, and there were brawls or duels or knife fights almost daily. The St. Louis of the early 19th century was an exciting—and frequently hazardous—place to live in or visit.

The trappers, known as mountain men, came and went in the midst of the commotion, and on their shoulders rested the burden of the riotously healthy economy of St. Louis, and, ultimately, the task of discovering the routes that would facilitate the impending westward expansion of the United States. Even among the colorful rabble of St. Louis, the appearance of the mountain men was remarkable. They were tough, rugged, weather-beaten individuals, with red, windburned faces, unkempt, shoulder-length hair, and long, heavy beards. They wore buckskin clothes, crude wool hats, and shoes of buffalo or deerskin.

The riverboat Yellowstone *moves past St. Louis and down the Mississippi River. St. Louis was the point of departure for westward travelers; it was also the center of the thriving fur trade.*

Along with crude snowshoes, their rifles or shotguns were slung across their back, powder horns and leather ammunition pouches hung from their shoulders, and pistols and massive hunting knives were held by their leather belts. Many of them bore physical evidence of the dangers and rigors of their trade—fingers or toes or parts of the nose lost to frostbite; scars from the bullets and arrows of hostile Indians, or perhaps the bullets and arrowheads themselves, permanently imbedded somewhere beneath the skin; or the massive scarring and tissue loss that resulted from encounters with the most ferocious inhabitant of the American West, the grizzly bear. The mountain men's capacity for endurance, their fortitude, and their fearlessness were legendary even in their own time, and they were regarded with awe by the less adventurous members of St. Louis society. A trapper returning down the Missouri from a fur-gathering expedition, which might have lasted anywhere from six months to three years or longer, was often greeted by a gaping crowd on the city's waterfront.

But the trappers were much more than simple, rough-hewn outdoorsmen. In order to survive and successfully exploit the unforgiving environment of the wilderness, they had to master and utilize a wide variety of skills. The mountain man was trapper, tanner, hunter, fisherman, riverman, cartographer, explorer, Indian fighter, frontier diplomat (it was always prudent to attempt to negotiate with the Indians before fighting with them), wilderness scout, venture capitalist, and, occasionally, international spy. He was perhaps the ultimate embodiment of the burgeoning American character—the self-reliant individualist, the relentlessly westering expansionist, and the enterprising capitalist, all rolled into one.

On February 13, 1822, an advertisement appeared in the help-wanted section of the *Missouri Gazette and Public Advertiser*—"To Enterprising Young Men: The subscriber wishes to engage ONE HUNDRED MEN, to ascend the river Missouri to its source, there to be em-

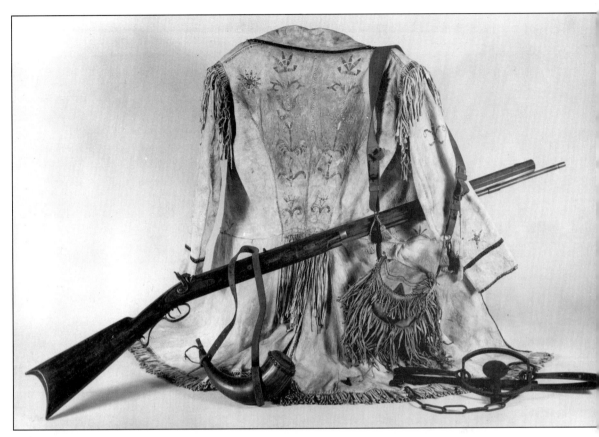

ployed for one, two, or three years." The fateful advertisement had been placed by St. Louis entrepreneur
William Ashley, who was in the process of forming a new
fur-trapping and -trading firm. In the years to come, the
"enterprising young men" who answered the ad would
become the mountain men of western legend; they would
also risk their lives in an ongoing attempt to penetrate and
explore the wild, unknown lands of the Rocky Mountains
and the Far West and to establish an American presence
there. But the story of the mountain men has its origins
back at the beginning of the 19th century, with the territorial ambition of an American president and the remarkable expedition of Meriwether Lewis and William
Clark.

*The mountain man's gear
included a long buckskin jacket
(the jacket pictured here features
elaborate porcupine-quill
embroidery most likely done by a
Crow woman), a powder horn
(for carrying gunpowder), a
leather ammunition pouch, an
iron beaver trap, and most
important of all, a rifle.*

Dear Sir   Washington. US. of America. July 4. 1803.

In the journey which you are about to undertake for the discovery of the course
and source of the Missouri, and of the most convenient water communication from
thence to the Pacific ocean, your party being small, it is to be expected that you
will encounter considerable dangers from the Indian inhabitants. should you
escape those dangers and reach the Pacific ocean, you may find it imprudent
to hazard a return the same way, and be forced to seek a passage round by sea
in such vessels as you may find on the Western coast. but you will be without
money, without clothes, & other necessaries; as a sufficient supply cannot be carried
with you from hence. your resource in that case can only be in the credit
of the US. for which purpose I hereby authorise you to draw on the Secretaries
of State, of the Treasury, of War & of the Navy of the US.. according as you may find
your draughts will be most negociable, for the purpose of obtaining money or
necessaries for yourself & your men: and I solemnly pledge the faith of the
United States that these draughts shall be paid punctually at the date they
are made payable. I also ask of the Consuls, agents, merchants & citizens of any
nation with which we have intercourse or amity, to furnish you with those sup-
-plies which your necessities may call for, assuring them of honorable and prompt
retribution. and our own Consuls in foreign parts where you may happen to be, are
hereby instructed & required to be aiding & assisting to you in whatsoever may be
necessary for procuring your return back to the United States. And to give more
entire satisfaction & confidence to those who may be disposed to aid you, I Thomas
Jefferson, President of the United States of America, have written this letter of
general credit for you with my own hand, and signed it with my name.

                                                        Th: Jefferson

To
    Capt. Meriwether Lewis.

The Passage and the Garden

In the opening years of the 19th century, the interior of the American West was still a region of mystery to most white Americans, and as such it represented the continent's final frontier. The eastern portions of North America, between the Atlantic Ocean and the Mississippi River and from the Great Lakes to the Gulf of Mexico, were long since explored and settled by French, English, Spanish, and American pioneers. To the north, the Arctic was still largely unknown, but practitioners of the British fur trade had explored and mapped much of southern Canada in the late 1700s, and the great Scottish explorer Alexander Mackenzie had crossed Canada in 1793. To the south, Spain had conquered the lands of Mexico in the early 1500s and most of North America south of the Rio Grande was well known, at least to the Spanish. To the west, sea captains from Spain, Russia, England, and the United States had provided accurate charts and maps of the Pacific coastal areas, and British, Spanish, and Russian fur traders had permanent establishments on the coast by 1800. Spanish colonists had settled the California coast, from San Diego to San Francisco, during the late 18th century.

But the western interior, the vast drainage basins of the Missouri and Colorado rivers, and most of the immense Great Plains region, were virtually unknown to the white

A July 1803 letter from President Thomas Jefferson to Captain Meriwether Lewis addresses the issue of financial backing for the Corps of Discovery. Jefferson clearly states his own objectives for the expedition: "The discovery of the course and source of the Missouri, and of the most convenient water communication from thence to the Pacific ocean."

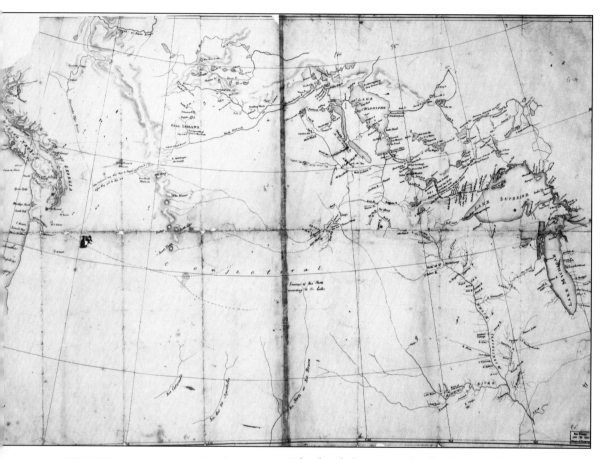

This 1803 map is an example of the extent of American knowledge of the geography of the Far West prior to the Lewis and Clark expedition. The most accurate label can be found just below the center of the map—conjectural.

man. The lands between the Rockies on the east and the Sierra Nevada and the Cascade Range on the west were also unexplored. The great Rockies themselves, south of Mackenzie's crossing in Canada, were still only a geographic rumor, and the eastern slopes of the Cascade Range and the Sierra Nevada were totally unknown. All in all, nearly one and a half million square miles of what is now the western United States were yet to be explored in 1800.

Americans filled the huge gaps in their knowledge of the West with, for the most part, rumor and wild speculation. The vast areas to the west were supposedly inhabited by fantastic creatures and strange peoples: Amazon tribes and communities of bearded dwarves were said to live in places with names like the "Mountains of Bright Stones" and the "Burnt Cliffs," and unicorns, mammoths, and bear-sized beavers (a trapper's dream!) were said to roam these lands. There were even rumors (circulated by no less a personage than Thomas Jefferson) of a mountain of solid rock salt "180 miles long and 45 miles wide." Americans' geographic images of the West were for the most part no less imaginative and no less incorrect, although some of them were based on realistic theories and were partially supported by the testimony of the few who had penetrated the fringes of the western wilderness.

By 1800, two basic geographic concepts were held to be fact. The first idea was that by way of the western river systems it would be possible to locate a water passage across the North American continent. This belief in a water passage was based on the theory that somewhere in the western interior there was a height of land, or common source area, for all the major western rivers. Locating the source area might allow easy transcontinental travel and commerce; goods transported upstream from the East could be portaged, or carried overland, a short distance to waters that flowed downstream to the Pacific. This "passage" would permit commercial travel from the Atlantic to the Pacific without the long and dangerous sea journey around the tip of South America, and locating it had been a prime goal of explorers in North America since the early 1500s, when Europeans first learned that a continental land mass barred their way to the Orient.

The second major concept upon which geographic images of the American West were based was the notion that the lands west of the Mississippi were immensely fertile and could support a highly productive agricultural civilization. Like the concept of the water passage, this idea of "the garden of the world," a kind of Eden just waiting to

More than any other man, Thomas Jefferson, president from 1801 to 1809, was responsible for making the United States a nation that stretches from the Atlantic to the Pacific. Jefferson's vision and ambition resulted in the Louisiana Purchase in 1803 and the Lewis and Clark expedition the following year.

Meriwether Lewis was Thomas Jefferson's choice as commander of the Corps of Discovery. According to Jefferson, the 28-year-old Lewis was "brave, prudent, habituated to the woods & familiar with Indian manners and character."

be discovered and settled, had been a primary part of the accepted geography of North America since the continent's discovery.

These two ideas, the passage and the garden, took root in the imaginations of Americans who were inclined to look to the west, and they would determine the nature of much of the exploration carried out during the first years of the 19th century. One of these westward-looking Americans was Thomas Jefferson, president of the United States from 1801 to 1809. It had long been a dream of Jefferson's to find the passage—a water route across North America that could be used for commercial purposes. And Jefferson's ambitions for the growth of the new American republic required a large amount of fertile agricultural land, just the kind of land that was rumored to exist somewhere on the frontier that lay west of the Mississippi. Jefferson was eager to set in motion the political doctrine that would come to be known as Manifest Destiny—the westward expansion that would ultimately lead to the establishment of an American nation that stretched from the Atlantic to the Pacific—and finding the passage and the garden would be a crucial step toward achieving this goal. Jefferson wanted U.S. exploration to begin as soon as possible, for he was aware of British exploration in Canada, especially Mackenzie's remarkable transcontinental crossing, and he worried that this would lead to British control of the Pacific coastal region.

In early 1803, therefore, Jefferson proposed to Congress that a small party of U.S. Army explorers—the Corps of Discovery—investigate the lands between the Mississippi River and the Pacific Ocean. Congress agreed to provide funds for such an expedition. Jefferson's personal secretary, 28-year-old Meriwether Lewis, was chosen to lead the expedition (the term *secretary* may be misleading; Lewis was an accomplished frontiersman, well acquainted with the rigors and dangers of the wilderness). Lewis appointed his friend, 32-year-old army lieutenant William Clark, second in command, and the two began recruiting the "robust helthy hardy young men" who would constitute the Corps of Discovery.

But before Lewis and Clark could begin their journey of discovery, a truly momentous event transpired—an event that gave their mission an even greater significance. In July 1803, French emperor Napoleon Bonaparte, in desperate need of funding for his European military ventures, sold the bulk of his North American colonial empire-to-be, an area known as the Louisiana Territory that included most of what is now the central western United States, to the U.S. government for $15 million. This epic transaction more than doubled the size of the United States, and Lewis and Clark were charged with the task of exploring these new American lands.

President Jefferson assigned three primary objectives to the Corps of Discovery. The first was to locate the commercial water route—the passage—from the Mississippi River to the Pacific. The second objective of Lewis and Clark was to obtain all the information they could about the native peoples and natural features of the newly acquired Louisiana Territory. Most important, they were to find out if the territory held the vast, rich agricultural lands—the garden—upon which Jefferson had pinned his hopes of American westward expansion. The third objective was to reach the Pacific Ocean and to claim the territory of the Columbia River for the United States.

In May 1804, Lewis and Clark and the 45-man Corps of Discovery left St. Louis (now an American rather than a French city) and started up the Missouri River in 3 boats—a 55-foot keelboat and 2 smaller dugouts. During the first summer and fall of their odyssey, they sailed up the Missouri River to its Great Bend in North Dakota. They wintered near the villages of the Mandan Indians, and the following summer they continued up the Missouri to its source in western Montana. From there, in a vain search for the headwaters of the Columbia, the party

William Clark, chosen by Meriwether Lewis as second in command of the Corps of Discovery, was the youngest brother of General George Rogers Clark, the frontiersman who, during the revolutionary war, helped to secure for the United States the territory between the Appalachians and the Mississippi.

trekked by foot and horseback 150 miles across the Montana Rockies, arriving eventually at the Clearwater River in Idaho. On the banks of the Clearwater they built small canoes and then voyaged down the Clearwater to the Columbia's major southern tributary, the Snake River. They followed the Snake downriver to the Columbia, which carried them to the Pacific Ocean, where they spent the winter of 1805.

In the spring the Corps of Discovery left the Pacific shores behind and began their return journey, pushing back up the Columbia and Snake rivers to the Rocky Mountains. Crossing the Continental Divide (the crest of the Rockies that separates the rivers flowing to the Atlantic from those flowing to the Pacific), they once again located the Missouri River. At this point the expedition split into two parties. Lewis and some members of the corps followed the Missouri downstream while Clark and the remainder of the expedition traversed a mountain pass to the Yellowstone River. New canoes were built, and Clark led his party down the Yellowstone to its junction with the Missouri, where they were reunited with Lewis and the others. Whole once again, the Corps of Discovery sailed back down the Missouri to St. Louis, arriving on September 23, 1806. They were greeted with much amazement, for the expedition had long since been given up for lost.

As far as the three objectives assigned to the Corps of Discovery by President Jefferson were concerned, Lewis and Clark could claim to have fulfilled the second and third. They believed that their glimpses of the seemingly endless Great Plains, as seen from the banks of the upper Missouri, confirmed Jefferson's belief in the existence of the garden. "This immense river," Lewis wrote to Jefferson in the fall of 1804, "as far as we have followed it, waters one of the fairest parts of the globe, nor do I believe that there is in the universe a similar extent of country, equally fertile, well-watered and intersected by such a number of navigable streams." Their evaluations of the quality of the

country west of the Rocky Mountains were less enthu-
siastic. Even so, they found several areas between the
Rockies and the Pacific that were, in their view, admirably
suited for cultivation by American farmers.

The third objective of the expedition was also accomplished; Lewis and Clark were successful in reaching the
Pacific Ocean, and in so doing they had established a
legitimate American claim to what was then known as
Oregon Country—the Pacific Northwest. Along with the
claim that was based on American explorer Robert Gray's
discovery of the Columbia River in 1792, Lewis and
Clark's reconnaissance of the lands between the Rockies
and the Pacific provided the United States with a powerful
argument for the rightful possession of those lands.

In achieving their first objective, however, Lewis and
Clark were less than successful. They did not locate the
common source area of the western rivers, nor did they
find a short portage between the navigable waters of the
Missouri and the navigable waters of the Columbia. This
was because these geographic features simply did not exist.
Nevertheless, belief in the passage persisted. William Clark
remained convinced that a common source area for western rivers existed somewhere to the south of the path taken
by the Corps of Discovery across the Montana Rockies,
and he included this speculative site on the maps he drew
following the expedition, thus propagating a geographic
fiction that was to vex western explorers for decades.

Despite their failure to find the passage, the journey of
Lewis and Clark and the Corps of Discovery was an un-
precedented success and an epochal event in the history
of the United States. The American West had been penetrated. The members of the Corps had endured dreadful
hardship and continual danger, but they suffered only one
fatality during their journey and returned to civilization
with a wealth of information, and, more important, with
wondrous eyewitness accounts of the West—accounts that
made the traditional myths and legends about the western

At the time of the Lewis and Clark expedition, the buffalo population of North America was estimated to be 60 million. The members of the Corps of Discovery encountered buffalo herds 25 miles wide.

frontier seem pale by comparison. They told of great expanses of rolling grasslands that teemed with game, including grazing buffalo herds so large that at times they seemed like a rough, furry tide engulfing the plains as far as the eye could see. They told of mountain ranges so tall they seemed to scrape the very skies, their peaks covered with snow year round. They told of glacial rivers and white-water rapids that stormed through deep granite gorges; of mountainous terrain as brutal and unforgiving as it was beautiful. They told of the many Indian tribes they had encountered along the way, some friendly, some extremely hostile. And they related hair-raising accounts of encounters with the dreaded *Ursus horribilis*—the grizzly bear.

But it was the descriptions of the beavers and sea otters seen by the members of the Corps of Discovery that had the greatest effect. The rivers and streams of the West were swarming with large, healthy beavers, it was told, and sea otters with magnificent coats frolicked along the Pacific coast. Here was a valuable resource just waiting to be exploited: A man who was rugged and brave enough to withstand the hardships and dangers of the western frontier might harvest a rich bounty in beaver and sea otter pelts. And so, in the wake of Lewis and Clark a new breed of men began heading west. These men represented the next wave of westward exploration, and their quest for virgin trapping grounds would enable them to eventually complete a detailed survey of the American West.

Lewis and Clark encountered the vanguard of this new breed of explorer before they had even finished their journey. On August 12, 1806, as the Corps traveled swiftly down the Missouri River on the final leg of the return trip, they came upon two men in a canoe paddling in the opposite direction. It was an unusual occurrence for white men to meet other white men this far upriver, so the travelers hailed each other. The two westbound men introduced themselves as Joseph Dickson and Forest Hancock, trappers from Illinois. These hardy individuals were bound up the Missouri on a fur-trapping venture. They had already spent two years in the wilderness, and despite repeated Indian attacks and other misfortunes they were pushing westward in search of beaver.

The two trappers were delighted to hear from the members of the Corps of Discovery that beaver were abundant upriver a ways, and they prepared to move on. One of the staunchest members of the Lewis and Clark party, a man named John Colter, wanted to accompany Hancock and Dickson, even though he had just endured two years of grueling hardship and toil in the wilderness. The trappers asserted that they would be glad to have Colter along, and Lewis and Clark gave Colter permission to leave the Corps of Discovery. The members of the Corps said their farewells to Colter and continued on their journey back to civilization. Colter climbed into the canoe with Dickson and Hancock and found himself headed upriver once again, back toward the mountains. The era of the mountain men had begun.

The members of the Lewis and Clark expedition and the fur trappers and traders who followed had frequent and harrowing encounters with grizzly bears. The frontiersmen came in contact with the ferocious creatures so often that they gave nicknames to the species; the bears were known collectively as Caleb or Old Ephraim. Meriwether Lewis referred to the grizzlies as "those gentlemen."

Colter's Hell

One of the first men to recognize the significance of Lewis and Clark's information concerning the fur wealth of the western rivers was one Manuel Lisa, and it did not take the shrewd Lisa very long to begin exploiting the information on a large scale. Manuel Lisa was a man of shadowy and dubious background; one of his contemporaries referred to him as a "rascally character." Of South American–Spanish descent, Lisa had moved up the Mississippi from his birthplace in New Orleans, settling in St. Louis in 1798, where he dabbled in the fur trade and the frontier espionage carried on between agents of the colonial powers. Terms such as *ruthless* and *mercenary* are often found in conjunction with his name.

In 1807, Lisa obtained financial backing from several powerful Illinois merchants and organized a fur-trapping and -trading party of more than 40 men, including the renowned hunter-tracker George Drouillard, a veteran of the Lewis and Clark expedition. Several other large-scale trapping expeditions were being organized in St. Louis in response to the return of the Corps of Discovery, but the ambitious Lisa got his moving first, and his keelboat and dugout convoy departed St. Louis on April 19, 1807. At the junction of the Missouri and Platte rivers, Lisa and his men encountered a solitary figure paddling downriver in a small canoe. This was none other than John Colter, the same John Colter who had, back in 1806, left the Corps of Discovery on its homeward journey in order to return to the wilderness with trappers Hancock and Dick-

Fur trappers and traders began arriving in the Rockies soon after the Lewis and Clark expedition returned to St. Louis in September 1806. Among the first of the mountain men to brave the harsh Rocky Mountain winter were John Colter and George Drouillard; both were former members of the Corps of Discovery.

son. Colter had been trapping and exploring the country around the Yellowstone and Bighorn rivers since then, and he was on his way back to St. Louis once again when he encountered Lisa's party. (The fate of Hancock and Dickson, like that of many of the mountain men, remains unknown.) And once again, Colter turned his back on civilization—Lisa hired him as a guide, and St. Louis would have to wait.

The expedition confronted its first real crisis—aside from the desertion of one of its members, who was hunted down and summarily shot by Drouillard—in northern South Dakota, where hostile Arikara Indians appeared and denied the party further passage upriver. Using threats and bribery, Lisa managed to ease his boats past the Arikara. (The next expedition to come up the Missouri, following two weeks behind Lisa, was not so lucky; it was attacked by the Arikara and driven back downriver to St. Louis.) Passing the villages of the friendly Mandan Indians at the Great Bend, Lisa continued on to the mouth of the Yellowstone River and then followed the Yellowstone upriver to its junction with the Bighorn River in south-central Montana. Here the expedition came to a halt. With winter rapidly approaching, the men chopped down trees and hurriedly built a crude fort of logs, which Lisa dubbed Fort Raymond after his little son in St. Louis. (It was also known as Fort Lisa and Fort Manuel.) Winter arrived, bringing subzero temperatures, howling winds, and heavy snows.

Fort Raymond provided a base for some of the initial probings of the Rockies by the mountain men. The objective of these expeditions was not primarily to explore new territory but rather to locate Indians who might be persuaded to bring furs into Fort Raymond, to be traded for valuables—trinkets, liquor, knives, blankets, rifles—brought along by Lisa. One of the men dispatched into the winter snows for this purpose was the indefatigable John Colter.

Colter was the prototypical mountain man—fearless, self-sufficient, durable, and possessed of a seemingly unquenchable thirst for adventure and danger. His solitary midwinter walkabout in 1807–8 would set the standard for the many mountain-man expeditions to come. Setting out on snowshoes from Fort Raymond in late 1807, carrying only a rifle and minimal supplies on his back, Colter trekked west across the desolate winter landscape of the Rockies. Living off the land, he moved through deep snowdrifts on the sagebrush plains of the Bighorn valley, crossed over the southern reaches of the Pryor Mountains in Montana, and hiked into a breathtaking mountain valley in northwestern Wyoming now known as the Sunlight Basin. Colter occasionally encountered friendly Crow and Flathead Indians, whom he encouraged to bring pelts to Fort Raymond, and he sometimes caught glimpses of less friendly Blackfeet, but for the most part he traveled alone by day, a solitary figure moving steadily across an awesome winter landscape, and camped by himself at night, with only the howling of the wolves and the brilliant stars of the western sky for company.

Trappers heading up the Missouri River for the Rockies had to pass by a large settlement of Mandan Indians at the Great Bend in the river, in present-day North Dakota. The Mandan were relatively friendly and were always willing to barter horses for goods brought upriver by the white man.

St. Louis fur baron Manuel Lisa
observes the construction of Fort
Raymond, built at the junction
of the Yellowstone and Bighorn
rivers in central Montana during
the fall of 1807. From here John
Colter and George Drouillard set
out on the first significant
mountain-man expeditions.

He pushed on, traveling south along the eastern edge
of the Absaroka Mountains to one of the major tributaries
of the Bighorn River—the Shoshone, located near present-
day Cody, Wyoming. Now he found himself in a fantastic
country of tar pits, boiling springs, and sulphurous gas
vents. This former volcanic region was so inhospitable and
desolate that it was shunned by even the most intrepid
mountain men of the future; it was given the name Colter's
Hell, and further major exploration of the area did not
occur until 1870.

Continuing his trek southward, Colter reached the valley of the Wind River, the name given to the upper portion
of the Bighorn. He followed the Wind River to its source
near the Continental Divide, crossed over the divide by
way of Togwotee Pass, and descended into the area known
as Jackson Hole. He was within sight of the Grand Tetons
to the west, making him the first white man to see one of
North America's most spectacular mountain ranges.

By now spring was on the way, and Colter had succeeded in making contact with Flathead Indians who were
eager to barter at Fort Raymond. Accompanied by a party
of about 500 Flatheads, he headed back toward the out-

post. Near Three Forks, Montana, where the Gallatin, Jefferson, and Madison rivers meet to form the Missouri, Colter and his Indian escort were attacked by a large force of Blackfeet. A fierce battle ensued, and Colter, fighting alongside the Flathead, was wounded. He managed to make it back to Fort Raymond alone, despite the bullet in his leg.

Colter spent the summer of 1808 recovering from his wound, and in the fall he returned to Three Forks to trap along the Jefferson River and to attempt to strike a truce with the Blackfeet. John Potts, another Lewis and Clark veteran, went with him. The Blackfeet were not in a conciliatory mood, however (they never were), and they fell on the two trappers. Potts was killed and Colter was taken prisoner. The Indians decided to have some sport with the mountain man; they stripped him naked and told him to run, and after giving him a slight head start, they took off after him. Colter, however, could run like a deer—he was renowned among his fellow mountain men for his fleetness of foot—and this he proceeded to do, bare feet notwithstanding. Soon he had outdistanced all but one of the Indians. As this swift warrior was closing in on Colter, the trapper suddenly turned on him, attacked, and killed the Blackfoot with his own spear. Then he dived into the frigid waters of the Jefferson and, concealed under a pile of driftwood, floated unseen downriver while the enraged Blackfeet scoured the woods for him. Once night had fallen, Colter came ashore and started running again, in the general direction of Fort Raymond. The Blackfeet picked up his trail and gave chase. Naked and starving, Colter nevertheless covered the 300 miles to the outpost in only 7 *days*. The men of Fort Raymond had seen many startling and incredible sights since they had come west, but none so incredible as the sight of the naked, exhausted, and malnourished John Colter, his feet leaving bloody tracks in the snow, running up to the gates of the outpost and collapsing.

The extraordinary John Colter crossed Wyoming's Wind River range during the winter of 1808. Traveling on foot and for the most part alone, Colter followed the Wind River to its source in the mountains and then crossed the Continental Divide via Togwotee Pass.

John Colter was not the only member of Lisa's crew to strike out from Fort Raymond on a scouting expedition. George Drouillard, the mighty French Canadian hunter who had been an invaluable member of the Corps of Discovery, set off alone from Fort Raymond in 1808. Initially, Drouillard followed Colter's southwest trail up the Bighorn River. But where Colter had veered west toward the Pryor Mountains and the Absarokas, Drouillard instead followed the Bighorn through the great canyon cut by that river across the northern end of the Bighorn Mountains. Traversing the high, arid plateau country (now called the Bighorn Basin) between the Bighorn Mountains on the east and the Absarokas on the west, Drouillard turned northward, crossed the high plains between the Bighorn and the Yellowstone, and followed the Yellowstone back down to Fort Raymond, where he arrived shortly after Colter's return from his misadventure.

Although Drouillard's journey was less dramatic than Colter's, it was nevertheless among the most important of the early fur-trade scouting missions. Besides being an unparalleled frontiersman, Drouillard was an excellent cartographer, and after his trek he consulted Colter and drew a crude map of their travels. This was the first map drawn by a mountain man. When the map was finished, Drouillard returned to St. Louis and presented it to William Clark, who was himself engaged in drawing a map of the entire West, which would be used to illustrate the journals of the Lewis and Clark expedition. Unfortunately, Clark viewed Drouillard's map as proof of his belief in a common source area for all the major western rivers because it mistakenly placed the upper waters of Wyoming's Shoshone River in the same vicinity as a river upon which, according to Indians Drouillard had spoken to, Spanish settlements were located. Clark assumed that this was the Rio Grande, which could be followed to the Spanish settlements of New Mexico, and thus he theorized that the Rio Grande's source could be found near the Shoshone's,

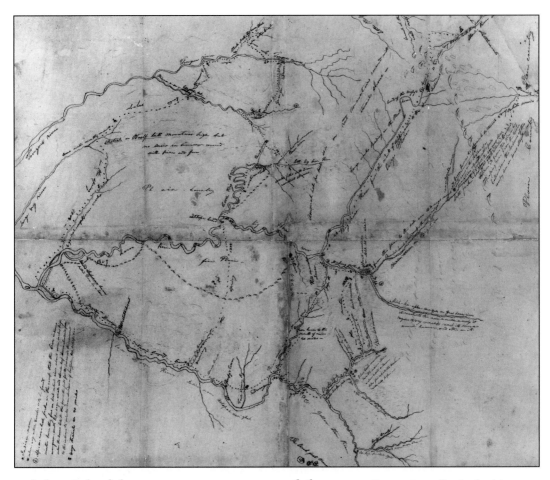

and the myth of the common source area—and the accompanying water passage to the West—was reinforced. In reality, the entire state of Colorado and the Colorado Rockies lay between the Shoshone and the Rio Grande.

While the likes of Colter and Drouillard were traipsing about the wilderness, Manuel Lisa had returned to St. Louis with an impressive load of beaver pelts and tales of opportunity in the Rockies (he played down the phenomenal dangers that accompanied the opportunities). Soon, Lisa had formed the Missouri Fur Company, a grand fur-trapping enterprise. Among the directors of the Missouri Fur Company were such influential men as William Clark

George Drouillard's final legacy: his 1808 map of the Bighorn and Shoshone territory. The map mistakenly gives the impression that the Rio Grande is only an eight-days' hike from the upper waters of the Yellowstone, a notion that was to confuse western explorers for decades.

Blackfeet Indians hunting buffalo on the high plains. The Blackfeet put up a fierce resistance to the encroachment of the white man. Many fur trappers and adventurers in the West—including George Drouillard—came to a violent end at the hands of the Blackfeet.

and Meriwether Lewis's brother Reuben Lewis. With the financial and political backing of these notables, the first Missouri Fur Company flotilla was launched in June 1809; more than 300 men, led by Andrew Henry, a former miner from Missouri, were carried up the Missouri River to the Mandan villages at the Great Bend. There, they were joined by Colter, who introduced them to the realities of life in the Rockies by leading them on a brutal overland march to Fort Raymond and then onward to Three Forks, the heart of Blackfoot country. A small stockade was built,

and as spring arrived the men began to venture out to trap the rivers and make contact with friendly Indians.

But Lisa's luck had run out; he had pushed too far. Blackfoot warriors and grizzlies took a heavy toll on the trappers at Three Forks. Drouillard himself was captured by the Indians, who disemboweled him and cut off his head. Colter was dispatched to St. Louis with a message detailing the woeful situation. This time, Colter met no distractions on his journey east; he arrived safely in St. Louis and delivered the message to Pierre Chouteau, one of the directors of the Missouri Fur Company. Mindful, perhaps, of the grim fate of Drouillard, the great Colter decided not to return to the mountains. He got married, settled down, and lived out the remainder of his days in relative comfort on a Missouri farm.

Colter and Drouillard were gone, and Lisa's enterprise seemed to be folding, but mountain men were still expanding the limits of the white man's knowledge of the Rockies. One of these men was the Missourian Andrew Henry, who had come upriver with Lisa's second expedition. Henry assumed leadership of the Three Forks outpost after Colter's departure and managed to keep it operational until the fall of 1810, when the trappers decided to abandon the post to the bears and the Indians. A number of the trappers then elected to accompany Henry across the Continental Divide to territory that they hoped would be beyond the reach of the Blackfeet. In the autumn of 1810, Henry led this party across the divide. Although they were harassed by Crow Indians along the way, they arrived safely at a fork in the Snake River—thereafter known as Henry's Fork—in eastern Idaho. A trading post (the first American trading post west of the divide) was built among the abundant evergreens of that region, but harsh weather, scarce game, and the ubiquitous Blackfeet forced Henry to abandon this outpost as well, which he did in the spring of 1811, retiring to Lisa's outpost at the Mandan villages. Blackfoot hostilities continued, and the

Missouri Fur Company men were soon forced to desert Fort Raymond. This marked the end of Manuel Lisa's first campaign to monopolize the fur trade in the Rockies.

As the farther reaches of Lisa's fur network collapsed, many of the trappers who had manned the outposts in the Rockies decided not to return to St. Louis or the Missouri Fur Company headquarters at the Mandan villages. Most of these remaining men dispersed into the wilderness alone or in small groups and were promptly swallowed up and never seen or heard from again. Some of them did reappear eventually, however, bringing tales of perilous travels. Ezekial Williams was one of the few to return from these ill-fated wanderings.

In August 1811, Williams and fellow trapper Jean Baptiste Champlain, with a party of 20, set out southward from the Bighorn, intending to trap their way to the Spanish settlements that they believed—incorrectly—were nearby. Williams and Champlain led the party up the Bighorn River and then through the Owl Creek Mountains of central Wyoming by way of the Wind River canyon. From here they veered almost due south across the arid desertlike country north of Casper, Wyoming, until they reached the North Platte River. At the North Platte, the party broke up. Some of the men turned back, and some followed the Platte upstream to the west and were ambushed and killed by Arapaho Indians. Williams, Champlain, and a third group crossed the North Platte and traveled south as far as the Arkansas River in central Colorado. Still a fourth contingent supposedly crossed the Sangre de Cristo Mountains of southern Colorado and made it to Santa Fe in New Mexico; whatever their destination, they were never seen by their former associates again. The Williams-Champlain group, in the meantime, was assaulted by Arapaho on the Arkansas. The trappers who survived the attack, including Williams and Champlain, were taken prisoner by the Indians. Williams managed to escape and he eventually made his way—after being held captive for a short period by Kansas Indians—down the Arkansas River to safety at a trading post in lower Missouri. Four years had passed since he and Champlain had set out from the Bighorn.

Ezekial Williams was the only man, as far as anyone knows, who survived to tell this tale. There were few who listened: Most people dismissed the wild story as the ravings of a man who had spent too many years alone in the mountains. William Clark apparently never heard the story at all; if he did, he ignored it. This was unfortunate, because Williams could have corrected some of the gross inaccuracies included in Clark's map of the West—especially Clark's belief that the sources of the Rio Grande and Shoshone lay close together. Williams had seen the Colorado Rockies and had traversed the central Rockies from north to south, learning in the process that it was a long, long way between the Shoshone and the Rio Grande. This information might have helped to dispell Clark's cherished myth of the common source region. Instead, it would be 10 years before the "rediscovery" of the Colorado Rockies by Stephen Long, an American army officer, and it would be even longer than that before Clark's imaginary geography of the common source area disappeared from American maps.

Despite all this, the travels of the first wave of mountain men, propelled by the ambition of Manuel Lisa, were crucial. John Colter, George Drouillard, Andrew Henry (whose career in the mountains was just beginning), Ezekial Williams, and others expanded the white man's knowledge of the mysterious West and introduced a U.S. presence into parts of the West not penetrated by Lewis and Clark. The first wave of mountain men had, in effect, gotten a foot in the door that had been opened by Lewis and Clark, and had prevented it from swinging shut again. The next wave would open the door a little wider.

Astorians

Manuel Lisa was not the only entrepreneur to under-
stand the implications of the Lewis and Clark expedition.
In New York, fur merchant and real estate mogul John
Jacob Astor heard the tales of the fur wealth of the Far
West and envisioned a great fur-trading empire, linked by
a network of trading posts, that would stretch from the
Missouri to the Pacific, and, Astor hoped, that would rival
the great British-Canadian fur enterprises, the Hudson's
Bay Company and the North West Company, which were
already active in the Pacific Northwest. By 1810, using
his own considerable financial resources, Astor had formed
and outfitted the Pacific Fur Company.

On September 8, 1810, Astor dispatched the 290-ton
Tonquin from New York Harbor. The ill-fated *Tonquin*
carried the first Pacific Fur Company employees—most
of them were French Canadian trappers and former
Northwesters, as North West Company men were
known—and the supplies needed to build a permanent
outpost, to be named Fort Astoria, near the mouth of the
Columbia River. The long voyage around Cape Horn,
then north to Hawaii and east to the Pacific coast of North
America was completed successfully, and the first Astorians, as Astor's men would come to be known, reached
the mouth of the Columbia in April 1811. It was here
that trouble began. In an attempt to guide the ship across
the treacherous bar at the Columbia's mouth, eight men

*Wilson Price Hunt, a resourceful
St. Louis clerk originally from
New Jersey, led a party of Pacific
Fur Company men up the
Missouri River in the spring of
1811. Hunt's final destination
was Fort Astoria, John Jacob
Astor's newly built settlement at
the mouth of the Columbia
River, on the present-day border
of the states of Oregon and
Washington.*

The doomed Tonquin *and two of the ship's rowboats founder in the rough waters at the mouth of the Columbia River in March 1811. The* Tonquin, *owned by New York fur merchant John Jacob Astor, survived this debacle only to carry its crew to a much harsher fate.*

in small boats were drowned. After the rest of the men who were to build the fort were put ashore safely, the *Tonquin* and its remaining crew sailed north along the coast to establish trade contacts with local Indians.

The Indians had other things in mind. At Nootka Sound, a large group of Salish Indians were permitted aboard to trade; once they were all on the *Tonquin*, however, the Indians pulled out concealed weapons and set about massacring the ship's crew. All but five crewmen were murdered; these five made a desperate stand and, using muskets and the ship's cannon, succeeded in driving off the Indians. That night, four of the men attempted to escape under cover of darkness but were captured and tortured to death. The fifth, a man named James Lewis, the ship's clerk, was badly wounded and could not travel; he stayed on the *Tonquin* and slept in the ship's gunpowder storeroom. The next morning, when hundreds of Salish came back onto the ship with plunder in mind, the clerk was waiting for them: He lit a match and blew himself, the *Tonquin*, and the Indians to eternity.

The Astorians at the mouth of the Columbia were horrified when they learned of the *Tonquin* disaster, but construction of Fort Astoria began nevertheless. Meanwhile, a second party of 60 Astorians had left St. Louis for the same destination—the mouth of the Columbia River. This expedition was led by Wilson Price Hunt, a St. Louis clerk originally from New Jersey. Hunt did not have much wilderness experience, but before he left St. Louis he managed to acquire the services of several seasoned veterans of the outdoors—former Northwesters Ramsay Crooks and Donald McKenzie, and frontiersmen Robert McLellan, Joseph Miller, and John Day. And, as he proceeded upriver, Hunt encountered six St. Louis–bound mountain men who had been part of Andrew Henry's dispersed Missouri Fur Company brigade—Edward Robinson, John Hoback, Jacob Reznor, Alexander Carson, Benjamin Jones, and Edward Rose (Rose was to become one of the most famous black mountain men). These six, in true mountain-man fashion, decided to forgo their return to civilization, and they signed on with Hunt and the Astorians.

In hot pursuit of Hunt's group was Manuel Lisa and a party of 20 men, who intended to overtake the Astorians and keep an eye on them; Lisa feared that these upstarts intended to move into "his" territory on the upper Missouri. There was a grand keelboat race up the Missouri in the spring of 1811, with Lisa's men, driven mercilessly by Lisa, gaining steadily on the Astorians. Lisa overtook Hunt on June 2, above the Great Bend. It was not an amiable meeting—guns were drawn and scowls and threats exchanged. The standoff continued until the two parties arrived at the Arikara villages near the border of present-day North and South Dakota.

Here Hunt made a fateful decision. He had originally intended to follow the route of Lewis and Clark up the Missouri to the Montana Rockies, across the Continental Divide to the Snake River, and then down to the Colum-

Fort Astoria, the Pacific Fur Company outpost at the mouth of the Columbia, proved to be an ill-fated establishment. Astor never earned a penny from it, and the lives of 65 Pacific Fur Company employees were lost during the first 2 years of its existence.

bia, the ocean, and Fort Astoria. But now, uncertain of the existence of a short portage from the Missouri headwaters to the Columbia headwaters, and well aware, thanks to the newly recruited mountain men, of the presence of hostile Blackfeet on the upper Missouri, Hunt decided to abandon the river route and instead to strike out overland due west to the Rockies. Hoback, Reznor, and Robinson were familiar with the western route that followed the Wind River to the Continental Divide at Togwotee Pass, where John Colter had crossed the mountains. From there they believed that they could lead the Astorians through Jackson Hole to the Snake River, and down the Snake to the Columbia.

The Astorians spent a month buying enough horses from the Indians to carry the expedition. (Lisa, relieved to learn that Hunt would not be proceeding upriver into Missouri Fur Company territory, assisted the Astorians in their attempts to purchase horses.) In August 1811, Hunt's party, which now included a pregnant Indian woman and her 2 children (the family of the party's interpreter), and 82 packhorses, set out overland, leaving the Missouri River behind.

During the late summer and early fall of 1811 they trekked west across the grassy steppes of South Dakota and Wyoming, through the Badlands and around the southern end of the Bighorn Mountains, and into the Wind River valley. Game was plentiful; the Crow and Cheyenne Indians they met were friendly (the Crow were so friendly that Edward Rose stayed with them when the Astorians moved on); and except for the occasional close encounter with one of the monstrous grizzlies of the region, this stage of their journey went well. The weather grew increasingly colder as they followed the Wind River west into the mountains, and near the headwaters of the Wind River they crossed the Continental Divide via desolate, wind-blown Union Pass, just a few miles south of Colter's crossing at Togwotee Pass. Once the divide was behind them, they proceeded west to Jackson Hole and then crossed the southern end of the Teton Range via Teton Pass, used by Andrew Henry in 1810. On October 8, in a driving snowstorm, they arrived at Henry's Fork of the Snake River; through the blizzard they could make out the Missouri Fur Company trading post built and abandoned by Andrew Henry a year earlier. The foot- and saddle-sore Astorians gratefully began preparations for their voyage down the supposedly navigable Snake. Canoes were built, the horses were left in the care of friendly Shoshone Indians, and the Astorians took to the water once again, expecting an

A keelboat moves past an Indian settlement on the Missouri River. Hunt's party, fearing the presence of Blackfeet on the upper Missouri, abandoned their keelboats in August 1811 at the present-day border of North and South Dakota and struck out overland.

After leaving the Missouri River, Hunt's expedition followed the Wind River through the Wind River valley (pictured here) in present-day central Wyoming. They reached the Wind River's source in the mountains in the fall of 1811 and crossed the Continental Divide via Union Pass.

easy passage down the Snake to the Columbia and thence to the Pacific. (Robinson, Hoback, Reznor, and Miller elected to stay behind and trap.) For the first 300 miles the going was so smooth and easy that the company frequently broke into song. Every day the current seemed to get a little faster, however, and on October 28 the Astorians found themselves being pulled downriver at an alarming speed. By the time the boiling rapids came into view it was too late to stop, and the canoes were sucked into a stretch of white water and jagged rocks known forever after as Caldron Linn. Canoes were dashed to pieces and a number of Astorians drowned.

The situation was grim. Further passage down the Snake was impossible, they were running out of food—game was scarce in this godforsaken region—and the brutal Rocky Mountain winter was about to fall on them in full force. They decided to split into two groups and attempt an overland march to the Columbia. Hunt led one party; Ramsay Crooks led the other. For both groups, this grueling winter journey was a time of desperation. Frostbite and starvation took a heavy toll. The two main groups split into smaller parties, which in turn divided themselves again. In the Blue Mountains, the Indian woman, Marie Dorion, gave birth. The infant died 10 days later, but Marie Dorion proved herself as tough as any mountain man and reached Fort Astoria safely. Hunt's party arrived in February, and Crooks showed up on May 1. Throughout the spring and summer of 1812, and even as late as January 1813, remnants of the westbound company continued to straggle up to the gates of Fort Astoria, which to them must have looked like the gates of heaven. Some of these survivors had gone insane, and there were rumors that cannibalism had been resorted to.

The Astorians at the mouth of the Columbia had had a rough winter as well; in fact, Astor's enterprise was in jeopardy. Food had been hard to come by, North West Company trappers had provided a stiff competition for the region's beaver and otter pelts, and the local Indians were behaving in a threatening manner. The Astorians needed to get a message through to Astor to apprise him of the situation. A young trapper named Robert Stuart was chosen to lead a party overland back to St. Louis. He would be accompanied by five men who had come west with Hunt and who apparently (and incredibly) had not yet had their fill of hardship and danger in the mountains—Benjamin Jones, Andre Valle, François Leclairc, Robert McLellan, and Ramsay Crooks. The journey of Stuart's party would prove to be one of the most important of the mountain-man expeditions.

They set out on horseback in June 1812, retracing Hunt's route back up the Columbia to the Blue Mountains of eastern Oregon. Here they left the river and traveled overland through the Blues and across the tortured country on the west bank of the Snake River into southern Idaho. As they moved along the bank of the treacherous Snake, they ran into Robinson, Hoback, Reznor, and Miller, who were fishing the river in a rather downcast manner. The four mountain men had enjoyed a successful winter of trapping after leaving Hunt's westbound party the previous autumn, but in the spring, as they prepared to leave the mountains with their pelts, they were robbed by Indians, who left them with nothing but the clothes on their back. Overjoyed to see some of their former companions, Miller, Reznor, Hoback, and Robinson joined them on the trek to the Snake River. There, Crooks found the place where the Hunt expedition had cached some of their trapping equipment during the journey west. Outfitted with traps once again, Robinson, Hoback, and Reznor said goodbye to Stuart's party and happily set off to try and recoup their losses. Miller, who had had enough, continued on with Stuart.

The company, now numbering seven men, crossed the Tetons into Jackson Hole. Here, they abandoned Hunt's westbound route. Indians they had met along the way had

In the summer of 1812, Robert Stuart (pictured) was dispatched from Fort Astoria with a message for Astor in St. Louis. Stuart and a small group of trappers endured a grueling overland journey, arriving in St. Louis in the spring of 1813. The route they used to cross the Rockies— South Pass—would prove to be the gateway to the West.

spoken of an easy passage across the divide to the south. Miller confirmed these reports. Instead of crossing into the valley of the Wind River over the difficult Union or Togwotee passes, Stuart led his men southward up the Hoback River, which flows northwest to enter the Snake in Jackson Hole. As they moved south, disaster struck in the form of a band of Crow, who descended on the party and relieved them of all their horses. Without mounts, and with winter rapidly approaching once again, it became imperative for the Astorians to find the alleged southern passage through the divide.

Trudging along on foot, they reached the headwaters of the Hoback River and then traversed a gentle pass into the valley of the Green River, which flows south through Wyoming to become the Colorado. Following the Green River south, Stuart led his party along the western flank of the Wind River Mountains, whose towering, jagged peaks filled the eastern skyline. Then, on Friday, October 23, 1812, they reached the southern end of the Wind River range and came upon one of the most important geographic features of North America. Separating the southern end of the Wind River Mountains from a series of rugged mountains farther south there lay a 20-mile-wide stretch of gently rolling, grassy hills. This was South Pass, the gateway to the West. It was the best route across the Continental Divide anywhere between Canada and Mexico. A newspaper report of Stuart's journey, correctly predicting things to come, asserted that by way of this pass "a journey across the continent of N. America, might be performed with a waggon, there being no obstruction in the whole route that any person would dare call a mountain." The door that had been pushed open slightly by Colter, Drouillard, and Henry, was now kicked wide by Robert Stuart and the eastbound Astorians. Stuart and his men crossed South Pass and came to the headwaters of the Sweetwater River, still in level grassland country, where they spent part of the fall of 1812. Fearing the winter

(continued on page 57)

The Hands of the Creator

Portrait of Antoine. *Antoine Clement was a mountain man who accompanied Miller on his western journey.*

The Mountains of the Wind, Devil's Gate, Chimney Rock; the Crow, the Blackfeet, and the Snake Indians; "Peg Leg" Smith; "Five Scalps" Rose; "Broken Hand" Fitzpatrick; the rendezvous, the buffalo hunt—these were some of the names and terms that made their way from the Rockies back east during the era of the mountain men. For most Americans, these words had to suffice, for until 1837 there were few true images of the Rocky Mountains to fulfill the expectations to which this colorful language gave rise. The only way to actually see the western mountains and their exotic inhabitants was to go there, and the few who could manage such an odyssey were always struck by the inadequacy of any words, no matter how descriptive—"I had heard and read of such things," a traveler wrote of his first visit to the Rockies, "but here was the reality far exceeding in its naked truth the romantic exaggeration of the novelist."

In 1837, Baltimore artist Alfred Jacob Miller packed paints, brushes, charcoal, and canvas and got to the heart of the matter. His travels throughout the Rockies resulted in 18 large oil paintings and almost 200 smaller watercolors, the first true-life depictions of the mountain men and their world to reach the public eye. On the following pages is a selection of Miller's Rocky Mountain work, featuring trappers, traders, and Indians, the buffalo hunt and the rendezvous, and the overpowering landscape itself. Charged with a high romanticism, the paintings communicate the awe Miller experienced as he portrayed a part of America that seemed, in his own words, to be "as fresh and beautiful as if from the hands of the Creator."

Crow on the Lookout

Buffalo Hunt

Jim Bridger in Armour at Green River
Rendezvous. *Bridger can be seen on horseback
clowning about in a suit of armor given to him
by a Scottish nobleman.*

The Halt

The Storm

(continued from page 48)
snows and high winds of this open flatland region, in December the party followed the Sweetwater to its junction with the North Platte River. They followed that river downstream to its junction with the South Platte, where they spent the rest of the debilitating winter, far out on the vast, snow-swept plains of central Nebraska. In the spring of 1813 they continued their journey down the Platte to its junction with the Missouri. They reached St. Louis on April 30, 1813. A prominent historian has written of their return that "the whole city turned out at the water's edge to greet them. It was like a second coming of the Great Captains Lewis and Clark." And indeed, the epic journey of Robert Stuart's company was almost equal in importance to the expedition of the Corps of Discovery, for the path they had blazed from West to East—the Oregon Trail—would ultimately be used by thousands upon thousands of westbound Americans.

Wagon trains move through South Pass during the great westward migration of the 1840s. The discovery of South Pass—located in the southern reaches of the Wind River range in present-day central Wyoming—was the single most important contribution of the mountain men.

The success of Stuart's journey did not help to keep the failing Pacific Fur Company afloat, however. The War of 1812 was breaking out, and because of the dominance of the British navy in northwestern waters, Fort Astoria was sold to the North West Company on October 16, 1813, and soon after it was occupied by British soldiers and re-named Fort George. John Jacob Astor's grand enterprise had failed. The Astorians themselves, like the members of Lisa's company, scattered in all directions. Many of them joined the North West Company. Wilson Price Hunt, through a series of improbable events, found him-self stranded in Hawaii. Edward Rose became an honorary chief of a Crow tribe and took many Indian wives. Robert Stuart and the indomitable Ramsay Crooks joined Astor's American Fur Company operation on the Great Lakes. The three inseparable Kentuckians, Edward Robinson, John Hoback, and Jacob Reznor, along with Marie Do-rion, her husband, Pierre, and their two children, joined a trapping party bound for the Boise River in Idaho. Dur-ing the winter of 1814 they were attacked by Indians. Robinson, Hoback, Reznor, and Pierre Dorion were killed, as was everyone else in the party except for Marie Dorion and her children, who escaped on a horse. They eventually settled in Oregon Country.

Although the travels of the Astorians failed to fully de-bunk William Clark's theory of a common source area for all the western rivers—American maps of the 1810–20 period still showed the sources of the Missouri, Yellow-stone, Arkansas, Rio Grande, Colorado, Multnomah, and Snake in close proximity—they had demonstrated that the best way across the continent was not the route taken by Lewis and Clark. Most important, they had raised the possibility that the best way across the continent might not be by water at all. Americans began to suspect that the most viable route might involve a lengthy overland journey from St. Louis up to the Platte River and then across the

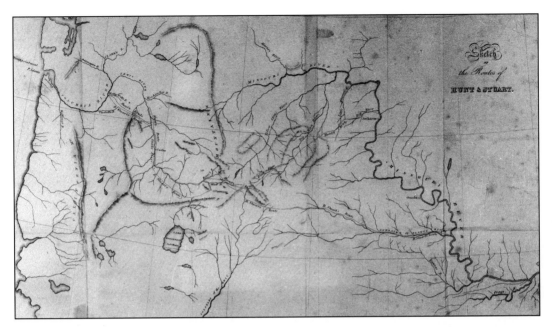

Great Plains to South Pass. This route would still follow the rivers because a source of water was necessary in crossing the dry regions of the West. But following the rivers was not the same as navigating them. After the explorations of Hunt, Stuart, and the other Astorians, Americans no longer thought seriously of sailing from St. Louis to the Pacific with only a short portage overland, and Thomas Jefferson's dream of a "water route across the continent for the purposes of commerce" began to seem like just that—a dream. The Astorians' travels also began the erosion of the old "Garden of the World" myth. When their reports of the hardships and dangers of travel across the grasslands of the Great Plains and the mountains farther west began to circulate, the mirage of a great agricultural paradise began to fade. Meriwether Lewis may have described the country around the upper Missouri as "one of the fairest parts of the globe," but it is doubtful that Wilson Price Hunt, Robert Stuart, or any of the other Astorians would have agreed with this appraisal.

Despite the collapse of Fort Astoria and the demise of the Pacific Fur Company, the two great journeys of the Astorians— Wilson Price Hunt's westward odyssey and Robert Stuart's eastward march—established the precedent of an overland passage to and from the Far West and pioneered the route by which such a journey could most easily be completed.

Northwesters and Taos Trappers

In the decade following the explorations carried out by Manuel Lisa's employees and by the Astorians, there was a lull in the activities of the mountain men. The two major reasons for this were the ongoing international dispute between Great Britain, Spain, and the United States over territorial claims in the West and the rise of Indian hostility in the Missouri River basin, which prevented trappers and traders from moving freely into the West via their traditional route up the Missouri. In spite of these problems, however, there were some tentative probings into the Southwest as a few American companies attempted to open trade routes between St. Louis and Santa Fe. There was also some activity in the Northwest, as the British-Canadian fur companies moved to consolidate the control they had gained over the Columbia River basin after the outbreak of the War of 1812 and the collapse of the Astorians.

One morning in October 1813 the Pacific Fur Company employees at Fort Astoria awoke to find the outpost surrounded by more than 100 rough-looking North West Company men. The leader of this force, John George McTavish, informed the occupants of Fort Astoria that because the United States and Great Britain were officially at war, Fort Astoria, being in disputed territory, had been claimed by the North West Company for Great Britain. Several Royal Navy men-of-war were on their way to the mouth of the Columbia, McTavish added, so resistance would be futile and the Astorians might as well turn the outpost over to the Northwesters now.

A Hudson's Bay Company trading post in Oregon Country. In the absence of American trapping or trading activity west of the Rockies following the withdrawal of the Astorians, the British-Canadian company had a free hand in the Northwest and set up trading posts as far east as Montana's Clark Fork River.

The Astorians considered this news. The situation seemed hopeless; they were outnumbered and would be completely outgunned once the British warships arrived; they had neither heard from Astor nor received any new supplies for almost a year; and, because most of them were Canadians and former Northwesters themselves, they saw no reason to risk their lives defending the American flag. A decision was reached: Rather than fight, the Astorians proposed, they would sell Fort Astoria to the North West Company representatives. McTavish liked the idea, and on October 16, 1813, Fort Astoria was sold to the North West Company, lock, stock, and barrel, for $40,000. The Astorians had no right to sell John Jacob Astor's property to anyone, but this did not bother them in the least—most of them hated Astor, who was by all accounts an extremely unpleasant man—nor did it stop them from dividing and pocketing the $40,000. After the deal was finalized, the Northwesters and the Astorians threw a big party. When

The massive, robust Donald McKenzie, a mercenary trapper-trader who worked for Astor, the North West Company, and the Hudson's Bay Company during his long career in the Northwest, revolutionized the trapping business by eliminating the Indians as fur collectors and replacing them with roving brigades of white trappers.

Astor himself got wind of this "transaction," he was un-
derstandably appalled. "While I breathe and so long as I
have a dollar to spend," he blustered, "I shall pursue a
course to have our injuries repaired!"

Meanwhile, the Northwesters had occupied Fort Astoria
and the Union Jack was flying above its gates. Some of
the Astorians departed, but many of them, former
Northwesters who had been lured into Astor's employ by
promises of higher wages, now followed the most convenient course of action—they rejoined the North West Company. One of these pragmatic men was Donald McKenzie.
Even among the host of colorful and outlandish characters
who populated the West during the mountain-man era,
Donald McKenzie stood out. A Canadian, McKenzie is
often described as "bearlike," and even "elephantine," for
he weighed well over 300 pounds. McKenzie was stout in
mind and heart as well as body, seemingly oblivious to
the hardships and hazards of a wilderness existence. He
was unintimidated by white-water rapids, unmoved by
subzero temperatures, unimpressed by grizzly bears, un-
concerned with blizzards, and unafraid of warlike Indians
(he once scared off a party of hostile Shoshone by holding
a lit match over a keg of gunpowder). He was also a shrewd
businessman, with a gift for innovation and for turning a
profit. Originally a Northwester, he had joined the Pacific
Fur Company in time to take part in Wilson Price Hunt's
overland expedition. After the sale of Fort Astoria he rejoined the North West Company, and soon he was put
in charge of all operations in the Pacific Northwest.

Between 1816 and 1819, McKenzie and his men engaged in intensive exploration of that region described cov-
etously by its would-be British-Canadian proprietors as
"the inland empire"—the area between the western slopes
of the Rocky Mountains and the eastern slopes of the
Cascades. Lewis and Clark, Henry and Drouillard, and
Hunt and Stuart had passed through the inland empire;
now McKenzie and his Northwesters executed a more in-

The interior of a Hudson's Bay Company trading post. Among the items traded to the Indians of the Northwest for beaver pelts were knives, blankets, axheads, gunpowder, rifles, ammunition, and whiskey.

depth reconnaissance of the region. Traveling mostly by canoe, with the massive McKenzie seated grandly in the rear, they extended the grasping arms of the North West Company into the interior.

In 1816, they reached the present-day location of Spokane, Washington. Two years later, they built a trading post near the junction of the Columbia and Snake rivers. From there they began to push eastward to the Boise River in Idaho and southeast to the barren sagebrush flats and rugged hills between the Snake and Green rivers, finding vast regions as yet unknown to the white man and, to McKenzie's delight, teeming with beaver. In 1819, McKenzie's men trapped as far south as the Bear Lake region of northern Utah. They did not discover the Great Salt Lake, which lay only a short distance to the south of their route, but in reaching the Great Salt Lake region,

McKenzie's Northwesters closed the gap that had existed since the 18th century between the Spanish penetration northward from Mexico into the Great Basin and the British and American explorations of the northern Rockies.

The travels of Donald McKenzie and his Northwesters resulted in the accumulation of geographic information that proved to be a valuable supplement to the already existing fund of knowledge about the West. The British fur barons who owned the North West Company also reaped the financial rewards of McKenzie's work. But McKenzie's most long-lasting and important contribution to the fur trade and to the exploration of the Far West was an innovation he made in the methods used by trappers and traders.

A Rocky Mountain Indian's painting of the hallucinogenic effects of the "whiskey" the Indians obtained from trappers for furs. The exchange takes place in the upper half of the drawing with the Indian on the right; in the lower left corner, the Indian begins to shake and see strange sights after sampling the booze.

Although some members of the fur companies trapped and skinned beaver themselves, as did the occasional free-lance trapper, the traditional fur-harvesting method used in North America, ever since the French began exploiting the fur resources of the St. Lawrence Valley in the 16th century, was to go into fur country, build a trading post, and wait there for Indians to bring in furs to be traded for items of European manufacture. McKenzie concluded that the fur trade could be made more profitable by elim-inating the middlemen; that is, by eliminating the Indians as part of the process. Instead of building posts for trading purposes, McKenzie suggested that the North West Com-pany employ its fur brigades not in trading but in trapping. Trappers would go into the mountains and valleys of the West and trap and gather for themselves the fur of the beaver, rather than depending upon Indians to do the work of collecting. These trappers would be paid fixed wages for their work.

William Wolfskill, originally from Kentucky, was one of the Taos trappers, a particularly tough brand of men operating in the American Southwest. The Taos trappers were among the first to penetrate southern California; many of them, including Wolfskill, obtained Mexican citizenship and settled there permanently.

This innovation, aside from being immensely profitable for the fur merchants, had a dramatic effect on the progress of the white man's exploration of the West. (The Indians, for their part, were probably better off not participating in the commerce, because the currency used by fur companies in their trading with the Indians was primarily rotgut alcohol. The alcohol, which had arrived in the West with the first white men, had a ruinous effect on Indian society.) Now, instead of a few solitary mountain men seeking Indians with whom to trade, fur brigades made up of large numbers of trappers began to invade beaver country. In their relentless quest for new streams and rivers to exploit and the best routes over which to carry their catch, this new wave of trappers would continue the process of unraveling the Far West's geographic secrets.

While Donald McKenzie and his men were at work in the Northwest, American merchants in St. Louis were engaged in the initial efforts to open up what later became known as the Santa Fe Trail, an overland route between St. Louis and Santa Fe that enabled American goods from St. Louis to be profitably exchanged for silver from the mines of New Mexico. When Mexican independence was achieved in 1821, the old Spanish ban against trade between the "internal provinces" of New Spain and the Americans ended. The Santa Fe trade began in earnest, and a thriving commerce developed between St. Louis and the Southwest. And inevitably, sometimes alone and sometimes in the company of trader caravans on the Santa Fe Trail, there came American fur trappers. The beaver resources of the Southwest soon began to diminish, but at the same time the lands around the southern reaches of the Rocky Mountains were becoming more familiar, first to the trappers, then to cartographers.

As the trade between St. Louis and Santa Fe flourished, American trappers moved into Santa Fe and a small adobe village named Taos. From these bases, they ventured into the surrounding mountains and valleys in search of furs.

Known as "Taos trappers," they adopted the new fur-gathering strategies developed by Donald McKenzie. Once they had a sufficient pelt harvest, they would return to Santa Fe or Taos, where they sold the furs to merchants who had followed the Santa Fe Trail from St. Louis. Among the Taos trappers were some of the greatest personalities in the annals of the mountain men.

One of the first of the well-known Taos trappers was William Wolfskill. In 1821, Wolfskill and a small party of hard-bitten trappers plied beaver-rich rivers, creeks, and streams as far east as El Paso and as far west and north as the Chama River and San Juan River country of northwestern New Mexico. The following year they worked their way north into the Colorado Rockies. Wolfskill retired briefly from the field to sell his furs in 1824, but in that same year as many as five separate parties of Taos trappers, including one led by the redoubtable Ewing Young, traveled north and west through the Colorado Rockies to the Green River, possibly even trapping in the Great Basin streams that flowed from the Wasatch and Uinta mountains into the Great Salt Lake.

Another of the 1824 expeditions was organized by a fat, hearty French Canadian mountain man named Etienne Provost, who led his party into the Great Basin and possibly stumbled upon Great Salt Lake. The Taos trappers were reaping enormous yields of fur by this time, and they were also helping to clear up some of the confusion that still existed concerning the locations of the headwater regions of the southwestern rivers, such as the Rio Grande and the Arkansas River. Wolfskill and Provost's travels in particular seemed to support the conclusion Ezekial Williams had reached a decade earlier—that the southwestern rivers had sources that were far south of the headwaters of the Yellowstone and Missouri. And yet the myth of the common source area lingered on.

One of the major expeditions of this period actually added to the confusion over the mythical common source

Etienne Provost was perhaps the most experienced of the trappers working out of Taos and Santa Fe, having spent decades in the mountains. Frontier artist Alfred Jacob Miller encountered the 55-year-old Provost in the mountains in 1828. Provost was seemingly indestructible; Miller attributed this to the trapper's considerable heft, writing that Provost had "a corpus Round as a porpoise."

area. This was the remarkable 1826 odyssey of a trapper named James Ohio Pattie, who chronicled his adventures in a popular book published in 1831, *Personal Narrative*— a rather mundane title for an extraordinary tale. Indeed, many of his contemporaries maintained that Pattie's story was simply too extraordinary to be entirely true, but Pattie himself was an extraordinary man, and if any of the Taos trappers were capable of actually making the journey he claimed to have made, it was he.

James Ohio Pattie, age 22, and several other trappers

were working the Gila River in late 1826 when they were attacked by Indians near present-day Phoenix, Arizona. Pattie and two others escaped and joined forces with another trapper brigade, led by Ewing Young. Then, if Pattie's narrative can be believed, one of the most incredible journeys of the fur-trade period was undertaken. According to Pattie, the Young party journeyed down the Gila River to the Colorado and then turned north up the Colorado to the Grand Canyon. They were the first white Americans to see this marvel. They took a quick look at the canyon, then continued following the Colorado northward to its source—the Grand River of the western Colorado Rockies. Then, according to Pattie, they traversed the western Rockies to the source region of the Platte River. Following the Platte northward, they allegedly reached the Bighorn and the Yellowstone, after which they followed a trail east of the Rockies back to Taos and Santa Fe.

Many people questioned the veracity of Pattie's account because he maintained that this journey took only three and a half months, which is indeed improbable. Pattie was not lying, however; he had simply misidentified certain rivers and geographic features, which led him to believe that he had traveled much farther to the north than he actually had. On the other hand, a lot of people believed his account, assuming that the journey had taken only three and a half months because the rivers of the Southwest (the Colorado and Rio Grande) and those of the Northwest (the Bighorn and Yellowstone), had a common source area. Thus the uncertainty over the source area was again stimulated. Nevertheless, Pattie's journey was a great one, for at the least he had stretched the reach of the Taos trappers into the region of the central Rockies penetrated by Ezekial Williams more than a decade before. And if any doubt remained concerning Pattie's honesty, fortitude, or his ability as an explorer, it was erased by his second journey.

Pattie spent the summer of 1827 repulsing Indian raids with his fellow Taos trappers, and in the autumn of that year he began his second epic journey. Accompanied by several other trappers and by his father, Sylvestre Pattie, himself an inveterate adventurer, James Ohio Pattie succeeded in opening a trail from Santa Fe to the Pacific— but the achievement cost him dearly. Setting off from Santa Fe in the fall, Pattie's small party followed the Gila River down to the Colorado, where their horses were stolen by Indians. The trappers then built rafts and went down the Colorado to its mouth at the Gulf of California. They buried their furs in the sand, turned north, and soon found themselves struggling across the desert, where they would have died of thirst had not a band of Yuma Indians rescued them. They arrived at San Diego in March 1828, where they were promptly thrown into jail for "trespassing" by Mexican authorities. Pattie was eventually released, but Sylvestre died in prison.

After Pattie's California trip, several other parties of Taos trappers made the trek across the barren desert country between the southern Rockies and the California coast. In 1829–30, for example, at least three large parties—one guided by a teenage mountain man, or mountain boy, named Kit Carson; one led by Thomas "Peg Leg" Smith, who was famous for performing the amputation of his badly mangled leg *himself*; and one led by William Wolfskill—journeyed successfully from the New Mexico settlements to California. Some of the geographic knowledge gained by these travelers began to appear on maps, but most of it did not. The Taos trappers, aside from Pattie, were a taciturn lot, not given to writing or even speaking overmuch about their travels, and hence, although the core of the Southwest—the New Mexico settlements and the southern Rockies—was somewhat well known by the end of the 1820s, most of the remainder of the Southwest was not.

While the Taos trappers were establishing a foothold in the Southwest for American commercial and political interests, the British Canadians in the Northwest were attempting to finalize the political and commercial supremacy they had assumed there following the withdrawal of the Astorians. In 1821 the long, bitter, and often violent rivalry between the Hudson's Bay Company and the North West Company finally came to an end with the merger of the two outfits under the Hudson's Bay Company banner. In 1824, George Simpson, the new governor of the company's Northwest operations, initiated a plan to keep American trappers from returning to the Northwest. The plan depended upon the activities of the Hudson's Bay Company Snake River Brigade, led by tough, resourceful Peter Skene Ogden. Simpson assigned the Snake River Brigade the task of rapidly depleting the inland empire of its fur resources. Simpson believed that if there were no beaver left in the region, American trappers would have no reason to come there. Along with taking all the beaver they could, the Snake River Brigade was to push as far south as possible while keeping an eye out for signs of American encroachment in the area. But no sooner had the Snake River Brigade begun to implement Simpson's plan than they were faced with the harsh reality that American trappers had come west of the Continental Divide once again.

On November 26, 1824, Ogden arrived at the Snake River Brigade's headquarters, called Flathead Post, located on Montana's Clark Fork River, where he intended to take command of operations. Just a few hours after Ogden arrived, Alexander Ross, the man Ogden was to relieve, returned to the post from the fall trapping expedition. With Ross were seven trappers, and as far as Peter Skene Ogden and the overlords of the Hudson's Bay Company were concerned, these seven were the most unwelcome guests they had ever received, for they were Americans, and their appearance at Flathead Post signaled the beginning of the end of Hudson's Bay Company supremacy in the North-west.

The seven Americans also represented the beginning of the next great wave of American mountain-man explo-ration in the Far West—the era of the free trappers. The free trappers were a new breed, a uniquely American phe-nomenon. They were their own bosses. They did not work for a company as wage slaves but trapped the beaver of the Rockies during the winter months and then sold the season's bounty to the highest bidder at an annual gath-ering of fur merchants and free trappers in the mountains, called a rendezvous. At these annual summer events, usu-ally held in the valleys west of the Wyoming Rockies, the trappers came together with merchants from St. Louis to exchange their furs for cash, for supplies, and for the "whiskey" called Taos Lightning, which was actually a mixture of grain alcohol, red pepper, and gunpowder, and which the trappers consumed in great quantities.

The free trappers were unruly, fiercely independent, prone to sudden violence, and virtually unmatched in their ability to survive in the wilderness. One prominent West-ern historian has described them as "expectant capital-ists"—in other words, opportunists who were in it for the money. But most of the free trappers only made enough money to allow them to buy the supplies needed for an-other season of trapping in the mountains; clearly, a good number of them engaged in this harsh and wild existence simply because they enjoyed it and knew they were suited for little else. There were still others, however, who had a vital understanding of their own importance to American interests in the Far West. These were the best and most significant of the mountain men, and their explorations would ultimately play a large part in making the United States a continental nation, stretching from ocean to ocean. One of these great American explorers was among the seven encountered by Peter Skene Ogden in Montana in November 1824. His name was Jedediah Smith.

"Enterprising
Young Men"

In 1822, the decade-long absence of fur-trapping activity on the upper Missouri finally came to an end. The foremost reason for this was the appearance of a personality with not only the resources but the leadership qualities and the will to set in motion such a perilous and uncertain venture. Not since Manuel Lisa and John Jacob Astor had such a man attempted to impose himself on the Big Muddy. But in February 1822, the riotous city learned with approval that there was once again a man in St. Louis who was willing to push an expedition up the Missouri.

Back in 1808, the year of Manuel Lisa's return from his first year of fur trading on the upper Missouri, an intelligent and ambitious young Virginian named William Ashley had moved to St. Louis. Ashley had a gift for making money. He was shrewd; during the War of 1812, realizing that the American forces would be needing gunpowder, he established a saltpeter (for use in gunpowder) manufactory in Potosi, Missouri. After the war he invested in real estate, and by 1819 he was ready to branch out further.

When Ashley had first come to Missouri, one of his neighbors was a man named Andrew Henry, the same Andrew Henry who, as a member of Manuel Lisa's Missouri Fur Company, had traveled beyond the Rockies in 1810. When the American fur trade died out on the upper Missouri, Henry abandoned that livelihood and became

An Arikara warrior. The presence of hostile Indians such as the Arikara on the upper Missouri was the primary reason for the decade-long absence of fur-trade activity in that region from about 1812 to 1822. This period came to an end in May 1822 when Ashley and Henry's first expedition got under way.

a lead miner. Over the years, Ashley and Henry became close friends; along with their other activities, they had both joined the territorial militia, and they rose through the ranks together (Ashley eventually became a brigadier general; Henry became a major). Ashley had always been fascinated by his friend's tales of the wealth to be made in the beaver trade; here, perhaps, was a great opportunity. Henry himself was aching to return to the mountains. In 1821, the two men formed their own fur company with the intention of reopening the St. Louis fur trade on the Missouri River. The partnership would prove to be a formidable one: Ashley was a charismatic leader with imagination, political connections, and great organizational skills; Henry possessed a wealth of invaluable wilderness experience.

The partners decided not to operate their new fur company in the same manner as their predecessors Lisa and Astor but rather to adopt the method used by Donald McKenzie. Instead of building trading posts and attempting to induce Indians to come to the posts and trade furs, they would send a brigade of free trappers into the field during the fall, when the beaver pelts were at their richest. The free trappers would collect as many pelts as possible and then winter where they might—with friendly Indians, or perhaps at a fort. After a short spring trapping season, the trappers would rendezvous during the summer at some predetermined site to sell their furs to Ashley and Henry and to refit themselves for the upcoming fall trapping season.

Ashley and Henry needed to get their enterprise under way as soon as possible, because three other trapping companies—Lisa's old Missouri Fur Company, the French Fur Company, and the Columbia Fur Company—were organizing to move up the Missouri as well. The first step for Ashley and Henry, then, was to gather together a trapping brigade, and it was toward this end that they placed their famous newspaper advertisement calling for "Enterprising Young Men." Among the hundreds of characters (some of whom would prove to be enterprising indeed, and others anything but) responding to the advertisement was a tall, wiry, blue-eyed young man of 23, who knocked at the front door of Ashley's St. Louis residence and politely introduced himself as Jedediah Smith. Ashley had no way of knowing it at the time, but this serious, rather pale and clean-shaven young man was to become, in a few short years, one of the greatest and most important of the mountain men.

Jedediah Strong Smith was born into a pioneering family in the Susquehanna Valley of southern New York State in 1799. In 1810 the Smiths moved to Erie County, Pennsylvania; for young Jedediah, this was the first journey in a lifelong odyssey that would take him relentlessly westward and that would not end until he reached the westernmost edge of the continent itself. In the Pennsylvania woods, Smith learned wilderness skills from his father, and he spent most of his time hunting and fishing and hoping to catch a glimpse of one of the vanishing Iroquois Indians of that region. He also received a good education from Dr. Titus Gordon Vespasian Simons, a pioneer physician who was a close family friend. This mentor gave young Smith a fateful gift—a copy of the 1814 edition of the Lewis and Clark journals. According to some accounts, Jedediah carried this volume, as well as a Bible, with him on all his subsequent travels.

By 1817, the Smiths had moved still farther west, to Ashland County, Ohio. In 1821, Jedediah Smith's westering inclinations finally outstripped his family's, and he left them behind for good. Moving steadily westward, he hunted in the Illinois country and then traveled down the Mississippi River to St. Louis. Here he moved quietly through the rowdy throngs, watching and listening, especially when he heard tales of the great Rocky Mountains to the west. Like most of the other footloose young men of St. Louis, he responded to Ashley's ad in the newspaper, and on May 8, 1822, he was aboard the keelboat *Enterprize* as it pushed off up the Missouri. Some of Smith's new associates might have looked at him askance at first, for he was not the typical frontier adventurer, being rather quiet and introspective and given more to reading his Bible than to drinking and listening to the more hoary members of the expedition tell yarns about Indians and grizzlies. But it would not take long for the young man to win the undying respect of every member of Ashley and Henry's company.

The famous Missouri Gazette *help-wanted ad of February 13, 1822, calling for "ONE HUNDRED MEN, to ascend the river Missouri to its source, there to be employed for one, two or three years." One of the men to answer the call was young Jedediah Smith.*

The *Enterprize*, on the other hand, won nobody's respect; in late May it was swamped and sank to the bottom of the Big Muddy, and Smith and his comrades were stranded. Three weeks later another boat, with Ashley himself aboard, arrived, and they continued upriver. In September they reached the fortified Arikara villages above the Grand River. The Arikara were unpredictable and volatile, and Ashley was as tactful as possible in his dealings

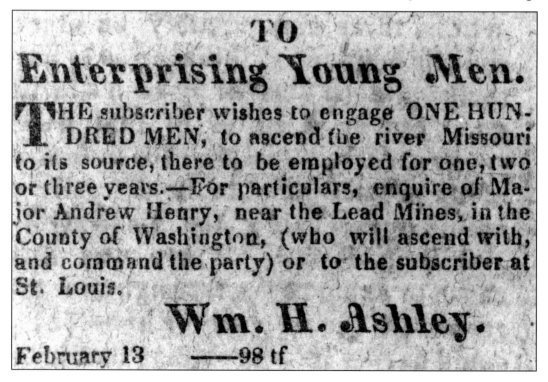

TO
Enterprising Young Men.

THE subscriber wishes to engage ONE HUN-
DRED MEN, to ascend the river Missouri
to its source, there to be employed for one, two
or three years.—For particulars, enquire of Major Andrew Henry, near the Lead Mines, in the
County of Washington, (who will ascend with,
and command the party) or to the subscriber at
St. Louis.

Wm. H. Ashley.

February 13   ——98 tf

with them, distributing gifts among the leaders and ad-
hering closely to the required nuances of Arikara etiquette
and ceremony. They managed to get past the villages without incident. Ashley then split the party in two. One group
would continue upriver while Ashley led the others overland to the confluence of the Yellowstone and the Missouri. Hopefully, Andrew Henry, who had preceded the
Enterprize upriver, would be waiting for them there.
Smith went with the overland party, and they arrived safely
at the Yellowstone on October 1, to find Henry and his
men engaged in the task of building what would come to
be known as Henry's Fort (later Fort Union). This outpost
was to serve as the first base of operations for Ashley and
Henry in the Yellowstone-Bighorn country.

During the winter of 1822–23, Smith accompanied Andrew Henry on some minor trapping forays, while Ashley
returned to St. Louis to recruit more free trappers. As
winter drew to a close, Henry realized that additional
horses were needed if long-range reconnaissance was going
to be undertaken in the spring, and he dispatched Smith,
who had already gained a reputation for resourcefulness
and reliability (as well as a reputation for being a crack
marksman), back down the Missouri to intercept Ashley,
who by now was on his way upriver with 90 new free
trappers. Henry instructed Smith to ask Ashley to barter
with the Arikara for horses; if they were successful, Smith
could bring the horses back overland to Henry's Fort.

Smith intercepted Ashley just below the Arikara settlement. They put ashore on a sandy riverbank near the
villages and approached cautiously. Delicate negotiations
were engaged in for an entire day. By nightfall, the Indians
had agreed to barter with the trappers. The Indians retired
into the village for the night; the nervous trappers slept on
the beach with their pistols and muskets nearby. The next
day saw a successful round of trading, but late that night
one of the enterprising young men was caught skulking
about the village. What this foolhardy person was doing

William Ashley's hopes for peaceable relations with the Arikara were punctured by a hail of bullets and arrows in March 1823 on the banks of the high Missouri. The trappers were routed by the Arikara and driven back downriver.

is unclear—some trappers later maintained that he had slipped into the village in search of a friendly Arikara woman—and he never got a chance to explain himself, for he was quickly killed and dismembered, and then his eyeless head was sent out to Ashley's party on the beach.

This had the predictable effect on the trappers, who began priming their guns and sharpening their knives. At dawn a wild firefight broke out. Ashley's men were greatly outnumbered and found themselves caught in an angry hail of arrows and musket balls. After 15 minutes the mangled party, leaving their newly purchased horses and many fellow trappers sprawled dead on the beach, beat a disorganized retreat; some took to the water, some took to the keelboats, and some ran overland ("I concluded," one of these men later recalled, "to take to the open Pararie and run for life"). The Indians stood on the banks of the river taking potshots at the swimmers and at the men in the boats, while other Indians chased the men who fled

on foot. Some escaped; others did not. The survivors re-
grouped downstream. A shaken Ashley asked for a vol-
unteer to carry a message to Fort Henry, and Smith stepped
forward. Making his way on foot across country that was
now crawling with hostile Indians, Smith delivered his
letter to Andrew Henry, who informed him that a party
of his trappers had recently been massacred by Blackfeet.
Ashley was learning (and Henry was relearning) a painful
lesson: The Indians on the high Missouri meant business.

These events had fateful consequences. Like Wilson
Price Hunt, Henry and Ashley decided to abandon the
waters of the upper Missouri. Instead, they would send
their brigades overland toward the Rockies. In the fall of
1823, two expeditions were launched from Fort Kiowa, a
tráding post safely below the Arikara villages. One party
would be led by Henry and was bound for the Yellowstone
country. Ashley, impressed by Jed Smith's conduct during
the Arikara battle—Smith was reportedly the last of the
trappers to abandon the beachfront—and during the crisis
that followed, put him in charge of a second expedition.
Ashley instructed Smith to push on past the Yellowstone
and to cross the mountains if he could. In late September
1823, leading a small party of about 20 men, Jedediah
Smith began his first great journey.

Smith led his men westward across an arid region of
South Dakota; it was so dry that the party often went 24
hours with no water, and men and horses collapsed from
fatigue and thirst. They passed into the desolate and for-
bidding Badlands, which one member of the party, James
Clyman, described as "this pile of ashes," and then into
the more hospitable terrain of the Black Hills. With the
possible exception of French traders in the 1730s, they
were probably the first white men to see this outlying range
of the Rockies.

Toward the end of their passage through the Black Hills,
a gigantic grizzly appeared and attacked the caravan. It
went after Smith and mauled him, taking the young man's

head in its mouth. By the time the bear had been driven off, Smith was in a bad way, with several broken ribs, a missing eyebrow and a dangling ear, and massive wounds to his scalp. Clyman got a needle and thread and stitched up the wounds as best he could, and the party halted its march so "the captain," as they all called Smith, could rest. Displaying remarkable recuperative powers, he was ready to move on after only 10 days, although he was permanently disfigured. As Clyman put it, this incident "gave us a lisson on the charcter of the grissly Baare which we did not forget." It also gave them a lesson on the character of Jedediah Smith.

From the Black Hills, they traveled across the Thunder Basin region of northeastern Wyoming into the Powder River basin. Taking beaver as they went, the company continued west and crossed the Bighorn Mountains into the Bighorn Basin, which Smith described as "beautiful, fit for cultivation, and filled with game." The weather was growing colder by the day, and they marched through a constant, icy wind as they followed the Bighorn River

In the autumn of 1823, Jed Smith led a trapping brigade through the Black Hills, an outlying range of the Rockies located in western South Dakota and northeast Wyoming. Here they encountered an encampment of hospitable Sioux, who invited the trappers to stay and rest for a while.

through its canyon in the Owl Creek Mountains, where the Bighorn becomes the Wind River. Following the Wind River upstream, they came to the Wind River valley, where they found John Weber's party—which had been dispatched from the Yellowstone by Andrew Henry—at an encampment of Crow Indians. The Crow were delighted to see Smith's party, for Edward Rose was with Smith, and the Crow regarded Rose with a mixture of love and awe; to them he was a legendary figure. (Rose was the embodiment of the term *free trapper*; he came and went as he pleased, joining and quitting trapping expeditions, fighting alongside Crow war parties, settling down with numerous wives in Indian villages, or appearing at a rendezvous, as the urge took him.) The Crow invited Smith's brigade to winter with them, and the trappers gratefully accepted.

Like the mountain man shown here, Jed Smith was attacked by a grizzly in the Black Hills. According to witness James Clyman, after the attack a mangled Smith told the trappers "you must try to stitch me up some way or other."

Smith wanted to get an early start on the spring march across the Rockies, so in February 1824 he led his men up the Wind River valley and attempted to cross the Continental Divide by Union Pass, used by Hunt and the westbound Astorians in 1811. But the Rockies would not admit passage, and the trappers were beaten back to the Crow encampment by a series of furious blizzards. Their Crow friends told them that there was easier country to the south, so they headed back down the Wind River and then swung to the southwest along the eastern flank of the Wind River Mountains. Near the southern end of the Wind River range, they came upon the Sweetwater River (a branch of the North Platte), which they followed westward to its source.

This was a brutal trek; according to the account of one member of the party, they traveled "westward through a barren land where their only water was secured from melting snow." The trappers endured harrowing, subzero nights when they did not dare to sleep for fear of freezing to death, while howling snowstorms and constant gale-force winds prevented them from building fires for days on end. Wrapped in ice-encrusted buffalo robes, they staggered through the snowbound valley of the Sweetwater. They were now starving as well as suffering from the elements, for they had seen no live game for weeks; it seemed that only they were foolish enough to be out in that desolate, freezing, windblown country. On the sixth day in the valley, Jim Clyman spotted a buffalo, and he brought it down with one shot. The trappers were so hungry that they could not wait to properly skin and cook the animal— they simply hacked it open with their hunting knives and gorged themselves on the raw, red meat. That night, traveling after dark, they found themselves trudging through a gently rolling expanse of snow- and ice-covered hills that glittered eerily in the moonlight. They did not know it at the time, but they were moving through South Pass.

Smith did not realize that they had crossed over the divide until they came to a river that was flowing west rather than east. This was the Green or Seedskadee (prairie chicken in the Shoshone language) River, which Smith recognized as "a Spanish river." By this he meant that they had come to either the upper waters of the Rio Grande or those of the Colorado—the Green is the upper Colorado—and now Smith understood that they were west of the divide. They had almost closed the arc of exploration with Taos trapper Etienne Provost, who was in the same general area at the same time. More important, Smith had rediscovered the easy crossing of the Continental Divide discovered by Robert Stuart more than 10 years before. For a variety of reasons, Stuart's discovery had slipped from the minds of cartographers and explorers during the intervening years, and the door to the west he had opened had been allowed to swing shut. Now Smith reopened Stuart's door, and this time it would remain open. After Smith's crossing, South Pass was finally—and permanently—recognized and utilized as the best way west.

Smith's brigade spent the winter of 1823–24 at a Crow encampment in the Wind River valley. The trappers considered the Crow to be the most impressive of the western Indians. The Crow were tall, strikingly handsome, courageous in battle, and expert horse breeders and riders.

A trapping party moves through a snowy pass in the Rockies. On a bitter March night in 1824, Smith and his frozen comrades found themselves traversing a similar natural avenue through the mountains—South Pass.

The party descended into the Green River valley as the first signs of spring appeared. The trappers were now in some of the richest beaver country in North America—before they decamped, the Crow had told them that beaver was so abundant in this area that traps were unnecessary because all a man had to do was walk around with a big stick and knock the beavers over the head—and the brigade split up into small groups and dispersed into the valley for the spring trapping season. Smith himself moved on to the Snake River country, where he encountered Peter Skene Ogden and served notice to the Hudson's Bay Company that Americans had returned to the inland empire. Smith was well aware of the implications of his presence in the Snake River country, and he derived considerable enjoyment from the obvious discomfiture it caused the fierce Peter Skene Ogden.

Meanwhile, the other members of the company had not been idle: Ashley and Henry's men seemed to be all over the Rockies during this period. They ranged far and wide, steadily adding pieces to the great geographic puzzle of the Rocky Mountains and the Far West. Some time during the Weber party's travels in between the late fall of 1824 and the early spring of 1825, Jim Bridger, who was to become one of the more celebrated of the mountain men, acting on a dare from one of his companions, followed the Bear River south all the way to its mouth at Great Salt Lake. Bridger may not have been the first to see the lake—Etienne Provost, out of Taos, may have reached it earlier in 1824—but he was the first to document its existence. (As reported in the journals of one of his companions, Bridger thought that he had reached the Pacific: "He went to its [Great Salt Lake's] margin and tasted the water, and on his return reported his discovery. The fact of the water being salt induced the belief that it was an arm of the Pacific Ocean.") William Ashley himself was engaged in his own exploration during this period, the heyday of the free trappers. In late 1824, Ashley left Council Bluffs on the Missouri River and began his pursuit of what was for him a kind of geographic Holy Grail. Ashley was intent on finding the Rio San Buenaventura, a particularly resilient geographic myth that had been appearing on maps since the Spanish explorations of the late 1700s. Supposedly, this nonexistent river flowed westward from Great Salt Lake across Utah and Nevada and all the way to the Pacific. From 1824 to 1826, Ashley led several expeditions in search of the fabled river; Jed Smith, back from his wanderings in the Snake River country and refreshed after a visit to St. Louis, accompanied him on the final journey to the Great Salt Lake region.

No Rio San Buenaventura was found, and Ashley, exhausted from his travels, returned to St. Louis, retired from the fur business, and went into politics, becoming a respected U.S. representative from Missouri. Andrew Henry had retired from the business a year before. Both men sold their shares in the fur company; Henry sold his shares to Smith, and Ashley sold his to Smith, David Jackson, and William Sublette. To Smith, Ashley left another legacy—the dream of the Rio San Buenaventura. During a series of epic explorations between 1826 and 1830, Jedediah Smith would pursue that dream.

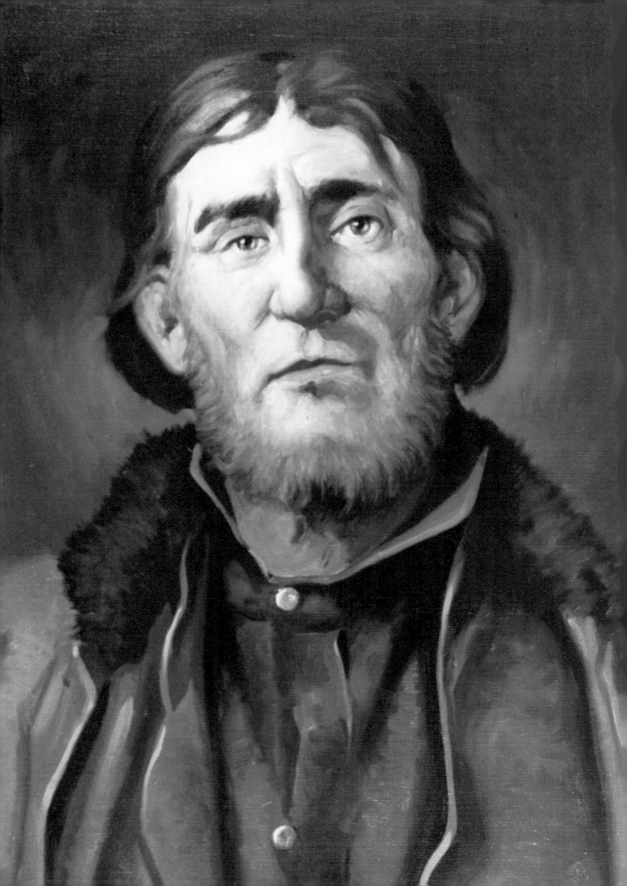

Defeat River

Who was the greatest of the mountain men? Many say it was John Colter, the solitary hiker who routinely traveled remarkable distances throughout the most inhospitable regions and who made a habit of extricating himself from the most dire circumstances. The Crow Indians would have undoubtedly said that Edward Rose was the greatest; they called him "Five Scalps," because he had single-handedly killed and scalped five Minnetaree warriors during a battle (Rose met his death—and lost his own scalp—on the Yellowstone River in 1833 during an Arikara ambush). Some might claim that Jim Bridger was the greatest of the mountain men. (Certainly Bridger himself would have said so—but Bridger was also known as the most prodigious and boastful liar ever to tread the fur-trappers' trails.) Or perhaps "Old" Hugh Glass was the greatest; Glass was once so badly mauled by a grizzly that his companions left him for dead, only to have him appear like a ghastly apparition six weeks later and hundreds of miles away from the site of the bear attack. ("Young man, it is Glass that is before you," he intoned to one of the trappers who had deserted him.) Lewis and Clark veteran George Drouillard could have made a legitimate claim to the title; his wilderness skills were unequalled, and most of the mountain men agreed that he was the greatest hunter and tracker among them. James Ohio Pattie covered as much ground and endured as much hardship and danger as any of them. Modern-day historians of the West often cite Joseph Walker, whose career in the mountains did not begin until 1833, as the greatest of the mountain men.

Legendary mountain man Jim Bridger was known to liberally embellish tales of his own exploits. "They said I was the damndest liar ever lived," Bridger complained. "That's what a man gets for telling the truth."

Walker, according to one of his contemporaries, was a man who "didn't follow trails but made them."

And by 1826, young Jedediah Smith had already accomplished enough to have his name added to the list. Among his fellow fur trappers, he was regarded with the highest respect. But from 1826 to 1830, Smith undertook an epic and harrowing wilderness odyssey that brought to his name a legendary status, and that made it clear that Jed Smith was unquestionably the greatest *leader* of mountain men to ever ride at the head of a Rocky Mountain fur brigade.

Smith, now one of the principal shareholders in the trapping firm of Smith, Jackson & Sublette, left the rendezvous site in the Cache Valley of northern Utah in August 1826, on what would come to be known as his Southwest expedition. With him were 13 veteran free trappers and a new company clerk, Harrison G. Rogers of Boonslick, Missouri. Smith intended to open new fur country south and west of Great Salt Lake. Once begun, however, this journey took on a momentum of its own, which would eventually carry Smith and his brigade all the way to California and the Pacific Ocean. Part of this momentum was derived from Smith's desire to locate the Rio San Buenaventura, which, according to William Ashley, would provide a watery highway from Great Salt Lake to the Pacific.

The Great Basin as seen from the summit of Tejon Pass in southwestern California. The basin includes most of present-day Nevada as well as parts of California, Idaho, Utah, Wyoming, and Oregon. Smith crossed the bleak wastes of the Great Basin in the late summer of 1826.

On the first leg of his Southwest expedition, Smith traveled from the Cache Valley into the valley of the Great Salt Lake and then south to Utah Lake. From there they traveled south along the eastern rim of the Great Basin to the Sevier River of southern Utah. They followed the Sevier River upstream through what Smith described as a "Country of Starvation" until they reached the divide between the Colorado and the Great Basin. They crossed over the divide to the waters of the Virgin River, near present-day St. George, Utah, and followed it southwest to its junction with the Colorado. They were now traveling through a harsh, weird landscape of bright red cliffs and odd-looking rock formations. The trappers had found no beaver streams throughout this long trek but only barren land covered with alkali flats, mesquite, and sagebrush. The heat was debilitating, water sources were scarce, and they were running out of the dried buffalo meat they had brought along for food. Exhausted and dehydrated, the horses began to die, and soon the men were on foot. They were greatly relieved to arrive at the villages of friendly Mojave Indians, near present-day Needles, California.

Smith and his men rested for 15 days among these gracious Indians. One of them informed Smith that he was closer to the California mission settlements than to his base in the Cache Valley, so the captain and his men purchased new horses from the Indians and struck out westward across the hellish Mojave Desert. After a brutal 15-day hike across country that was even more barren than the land near the Colorado, the trappers reached the San Bernardino Mountains of southern California in November 1826. Soon after, they came down out of the mountains into the lush San Bernardino Valley; this country, with its clear streams and rivers, deep green grasslands, shadowy stands of oak and willow, and huge herds of cattle, horses, and sheep, seemed like a paradise after the sterile, unforgiving desert. An old Indian led them to Mission San Gabriel, just east of where Los Angeles now sprawls across

At the Mojave villages on the Colorado River, Smith and his trappers enjoyed a welcome respite from the parched lands of the Utah region of the Great Basin. After a period of rest among the Indians, Smith led his brigade across the brutal Mojave Desert to California.

It was a severely debilitated brigade of trappers that arrived at California's Mission San Gabriel in November 1826. The Mexican authorities were less than sympathetic; they put Smith under house arrest and then told him to go back the way he had come.

the Los Angeles basin. Knowing that they were now in Mexican territory, Smith sent a judicious letter to the governor in San Diego, announcing his presence and requesting permission to travel north through California in search of furs. He also intended to search for the Buenaventura, although he did not inform the governor of this intention.

Smith and his men now encountered an obstacle that proved to be as difficult to surmount as any desert or mountain range—red tape. They remained in southern California for two months before they were finally given permission to leave by the suspicious Mexican officials. But, the Mexican governor told them, they were not to explore northward through California; instead they must cross back over the mountains in the direction from which they had come. Smith and his trappers had no choice but to retrace their route over the San Bernardino Mountains. But once they were back on the east side of the mountains, Smith, unwilling to recross the Mojave Desert, decided to turn north. Skirting the western edge of the desert, they moved westward over the Tehachapi range into the valley of the San Joaquin River. They were now in the southern end of the Great Valley of California, which lays between the Sierra Nevada to the east and the California coastal ranges to the south. Smith and his men were the first Americans to pass through the Great Valley, and here they found the first beaver streams since leaving Salt Lake. This was prime beaver country, and the brigade eagerly trapped its way northward along the San Joaquin, accumulating 1,500 pounds of beaver pelts—a major harvest. Once their horses were loaded down with fur they decided to leave California. They headed east to the Sierra Nevada and attempted a crossing in May. But the spring snows were too deep, and after losing several horses in the drifts, they retreated and made camp on the Stanislaus River. Smith recognized the difficulty of attempting a mountain crossing with his full party and their winter's catch of beaver, so,

leaving most of his men in the camp on the Stanislaus
under the command of the clerk Rogers, Smith, with two
men and a few mules and horses, crossed over the Sierra
Nevada south of Lake Tahoe, on the present-day Califor-
nia-Nevada border.

The small party then followed the Walker River downstream to the east until its waters disappeared into Walker
Lake. From here they struck out due east across the barren
deserts of central Nevada. Again they endured a grueling
desert march, running out of food and going days on end
without water. Occasionally they buried themselves in the
sand in order to escape the merciless sun. The horses and
mules gave out one by one, and the starving trappers ate
the dried-out, emaciated flesh. Smith recorded the con-
dition of the party in his journal: "Our sleep was not
repose, for tormented nature made us dream of things we
had not and for the want of which it seemed possible and
even probable we might perish in the desert unheard of
and unpitied." There were several times during this terrible
march when the men were ready to simply sit down and
die, and only the will of the captain and his uncanny
ability to locate water kept them from doing so. On June
27, 1827, Smith caught sight of the Great Salt Lake, shim-
mering like a beautiful mirage in the distance. It was,
Smith wrote, "a joyful sight, for we knew we would soon
be in a country where we would find game and water
which were to us objects of great importance."

Although they had failed to find the Buenaventura,
Smith and his men had done what no one had done before:
They had crossed over the highest mountains and the
largest desert in the United States. They had discovered
the rich beaver country of the central portions of California's Great Valley and had recognized the valley as a pas-
toral paradise that might accommodate hundreds of
thousands of American farmers; here, finally, was Jefferson's "garden." The Southwest expedition was a stunning
feat of endurance and determination. Fittingly, Smith's

San Francisco, where Smith was detained by Mexican authorities for two months in the fall of 1827. Smith chafed to leave the city and continue his expedition, but he would have done better to linger, for tragedy awaited him to the north, in Oregon Country.

arrival at the rendezvous encampment at Bear Lake on July 4, 1827, "caused considerable bustle in camp, for myself and party had been given up as lost. A small Cannon brought up from St. Louis was loaded and fired for a salute."

One would think that after almost a year of toil, near starvation, and constant peril in the wilderness Captain Smith might allow himself a decent vacation. But that was not Smith's way. He was a man who drove himself relentlessly, and while his fellow trappers were enjoying the kind of debauch that usually occurred at a rendezvous, Smith was quietly preparing himself for a new journey. Not 2 weeks after his arrival in camp he was ready to set out once again for California's Stanislaus River, where he had left a dozen men and 1,500 pounds of beaver.

On July 13, 1827, Smith, 18 men, and 2 Canadian Indian women (the wives of 2 of the trappers) struck out for California. Not wanting to again brave the fearful desert crossing of his eastbound trip, Smith followed basically the same route to the Mojave villages on the lower Colorado that he had followed the year before. But the Mojave, who had been so hospitable the last time, were not so friendly now. Indeed, in the year that had passed since Smith's first visit to the villages, their mood had changed from gracious to homicidal, for recently they had had some unpleasant encounters with white men. On August 18, Smith attempted to get his brigade across the Colorado. He had gotten half the party across when the Indians assaulted the others waiting on the opposite bank. Ten of the trappers were killed and the two women were taken prisoner while Smith watched helplessly from across the river. Smith and the nine survivors soon saw a large party of Mojave approaching on their side of the river, intent, as Smith put it, on terminating "all my measures for futurity." The sharpshooting trappers held the Indians off until dusk and then fled into the desert.

Smith had hoped to avoid the desert, but once again he was forced to lead his men on a grueling, thirsty march. "My men were much discouraged," he wrote, "but I cheered and urged them forward as much as possible." Once again it was only Smith's leadership qualities and resourcefulness that kept his men from giving up hope, and once again he led them safely out of the hellish desert, across the mountains, and down into the promised land of the San Bernardino Valley.

The Mexican authorities were less than happy to learn that the American trapper Smith had reappeared at the missions. He was threatened with arrest and then taken by sea to San Francisco, where he was interrogated by Mexican officials who were convinced he was a spy for the U.S. government. Smith spent two months in San Francisco trying to convince the Mexicans that he was simply a beaver trapper, which was difficult because most of them had no idea what a beaver was. Eventually he was allowed to rejoin his men, who had been brought north overland and who were in a foul mood after rough treatment by the Mexicans. At San Francisco, Smith was also joined by Harrison Rogers and the men who had been left the year before at the camp on the Stanislaus. On December 30, 1827, the trapping brigade was allowed to depart San Francisco. Smith could finally return again "to the woods, the river, the prairae, the Camp & the Game with a feeling somewhat like that of a prisoner escaped from his dungeon and his chains."

He still harbored hopes of finding the elusive Buenaventura. He knew that his route across the Great Basin to Great Salt Lake earlier that year had been too far south to prove conclusively that the Buenaventura did not exist. Therefore, he now followed the Sacramento River north into the Sierra Nevada far enough to convince himself that it had its source on the western side of the mountains and did not flow through the range from the Great Basin.

From the headwaters of the Sacramento, he and his men steered eastward toward the coast and began working their way north. Now they passed through a land that was the direct opposite of the desert they had endured earlier—thick, wet, almost impenetrable forests. It rained constantly. Heavy fog impaired their travel, and the horses moved with difficulty over swollen creeks and streams and through muddy sloughs and bogs. Although there was plenty of game and beaver here, Smith was uneasy. On March 8, Rogers was severely mauled by a grizzly, and on April 7, Smith himself had two unnerving encounters with the bears. Indians followed the trappers constantly and raided their traps or shot arrows into the horses. Smith or one of the others would occasionally pick off one of the Indians with a long-distance rifle shot, a practice that certainly did not endear them to the locals and that probably led to the grim events to come.

The constant, numbing rain continued to fall. In late June 1828, Smith's party crossed into Oregon and traveled north along the rough, fog-shrouded Pacific coast. On July 13 they reached the confluence of the Umpqua River and

Smith encountered the Mojave Indians again in the summer of 1827 at the start of his second journey to California. The Indians did not welcome Smith and his trappers this time, however, and killed half of them in an ambush on the Colorado River.

its north branch, where they made camp while "a considerable Thunder shower" spooked the horses and drenched the trappers yet again. They were now in Hudson's Bay Company territory. On the morning of July 14, Smith and two trappers paddled off in a canoe to scout out the area. Later that day, Smith returned to find his men butchered; a large party of Kelawatset had attacked the camp with axes and killed everyone in sight. A horrified Smith and his two remaining trappers fled to Fort Vancouver, a Hudson's Bay Company post situated at the place where the Willamette River joins the Columbia.

His men were dead, his horses, traps, furs, and other possessions were scattered—although some of his belongings, including his journals, were eventually recovered by Hudson's Bay Company trappers—and, in effect, Smith's expedition was over. It was a bad end to a great journey, and one can only imagine the gloom that must have enveloped him during the long winter at Fort Vancouver. In March 1829, Smith took his final leave of the Pacific coast, heading east toward the Rockies. For a long time after, the branch of the Umpqua where the massacre took place was called Defeat River. Eventually, however, it was renamed the Smith River.

It was a different Jedediah Smith who arrived at the summer rendezvous at Pierre's Hole in 1829. His experiences in the wilderness—and especially the Umpqua massacre—had changed him, and his years of exploration were over. He felt a new yearning to see his family again, and death seemed to be always on his mind. Smith's years in the mountains were about finished. He engaged in two more trapping expeditions, but aside from the territory inhabited—and still fiercely defended—by the Blackfeet, the Rockies were nearly trapped out. In the spring of 1830, Smith sold his shares in the fur company to Jackson and Sublette and left the mountains forever. He returned to St. Louis, purchased a farm, and became active in a merchant company involved in the Santa Fe trade. In the

Fort Vancouver, a Hudson's Bay Company outpost at the junction of the Willamette and Columbia rivers in present-day Washington State. A stunned Jedediah Smith took refuge here after Kelawatset Indians massacred his trapping brigade in July 1828.

spring of 1831, on a trip to Santa Fe with a caravan of St. Louis traders, Smith rode out ahead of the wagons to look for water, something he had done a hundred times before. The caravan was crossing an extremely arid stretch of land, known as the "water scrape," that lays between the Arkansas and Cimarron rivers, near the Three Corners area where Colorado, Kansas, and Oklahoma come together. While searching for a water hole, Smith encountered a hunting party of Comanche, a notoriously warlike tribe. One of the Indians shot Smith in the back. Smith managed to get one shot off, killing the leader of the party, before the rest of the Indians pulled him from his horse. One of the fur trade's greatest explorers was dead at the age of 32. His remains were never found.

In his travels from 1826 to 1830, Smith saw more of the American West than any man before him. He was the first to discover the overland route to California. He was the first to traverse the Great Basin. He was the first to travel overland from California to the Columbia River. Like many other fur-trade explorers, Smith died before most of the geographic knowledge he had gathered could be made public. Some of the journals kept by Smith were not published until the 20th century and others were lost altogether. Nevertheless, Smith's impact during his own time is undeniable. He wrote several letters to William Clark, U.S. superintendent of Indian affairs in St. Louis and unofficial custodian of information concerning the West, and the information provided to Clark by Smith quickly became part of the U.S. government's growing data bank.

One outstanding example of Smith's practical contribution to this fund of information was a letter that he wrote in October 1830 to John Eaton, the U.S. secretary of war. In this letter, Smith detailed many of his explorations. In particular, he described the rich country controlled by the Hudson's Bay Company in the Pacific Northwest and asserted how valuable the area might be for American farmers. He also described in detail the route to follow from St. Louis to Oregon Country—the Oregon Trail. A Pulitzer Prize–winning historian of the American West has called this letter "one of the most important contributions to a practical knowledge of the West ever made."

Some of Smith's geographic discoveries began to appear on maps as early as 1830, and although no map drawn by Smith himself has survived, several maps drawn between 1830 and 1845 show direct evidence of having been constructed from various maps drawn by Smith and presented to government officials and others. An examination of these maps provides a clear view of the contributions of Jedediah Strong Smith to an improved American image of the West. These contributions allowed mapmakers to draw the drainage systems of the Bighorn and Yellowstone rivers correctly for the first time; they also resulted in the first accurate representations of the Platte River route to South Pass and of the valley of the Green River west of the Continental Divide. The first representations of the Great Basin as a region of interior drainage appeared on maps derived from Smith's geographic data, and the first accurate views of the Sierra Nevada, the Great Valley of California, and the California coastal ranges also came from Smith. Finally, after Smith's exhaustive search, fewer and fewer maps showed a mythical Rio San Buenaventura flowing west from the Rockies to the Pacific.

In 1832, Jedediah Smith was eulogized in the *Illinois Monthly* by an anonymous admirer, who wrote that Smith was "a man whom none could approach without respect, or know without esteem. And though he fell under the spears of the savages, and his body has glutted the prairie wolf, and none can tell where his bones are bleaching, he must not be forgotten." Smith himself insured that he would not be forgotten, for every map of the American West drawn since his death bears the legacy of his courage, his perseverance, his vision, and his will.

The Last Rendezvous

The Rocky Mountain fur trade had reached its peak at the time of Jedediah Smith's death and began a period of decline during the 1830s. By this time the fur trappers had learned the mountains and plains and deserts from the northern Missouri River to southern New Mexico and from St. Louis to the Pacific. They had opened the northern, central, and southern Rockies for economic exploitation and had penetrated the Great Basin, Oregon Country, and California. But much of the geographic knowledge accumulated by the trappers had yet to have an effect on the popular American perception of the West. During the decade of the 1830s this began to change as people other than trappers and traders began to move into and across the mountains. The first missionaries, settlers, romantic adventurers, writers, artists, and new "expectant capitalists" of one kind or another began to arrive in the Rockies, and all of these people relied on the fur trappers' understanding of western geography to get where they wanted to go.

One western traveler who used fur-trapper lore to facilitate his travels was Benjamin Bonneville. Bonneville was a West Point graduate who took leave from the U.S. Army in 1831 to engage in the fur trade. There was much more to Bonneville than met the eye, however; most historians believe he was an agent of the U.S. government who, under the guise of "fur trader," was actually engaged

Joseph Walker was the last—and perhaps the greatest—of the fur-trade mountain men. He was "well hardened to the hardships of the wilderness," wrote a contemporary. "[He] understood the character of the Indians very well—was kind and affable to his men, but at the same time at liberty to command without giving offense—and to explore unknown regions was his chief delight."

The death of Jedediah Smith in 1831 marked the beginning of the end of the free-trapper era. During the 1830s, the role of the mountain man began to change; many of them gave up the fur trade and became guides and scouts for westward-bound settlers.

in gathering intelligence about the Far West that might help the United States gain control over the region. Intelligence gathering of a more public kind also began during this period, as American writers and painters discovered the Far West. One of America's foremost men of letters, Washington Irving, wrote an enormously popular book about Bonneville's travels—*Adventures of Captain Bonneville*—and this book played a major part in introducing the West of the mountain men to the common American.

Captain Bonneville and 110 volunteers set out for the mountains in May 1832 with wagon loads of trade goods and supplies. Bonneville used the now familiar fur-trade route up the North Platte and across South Pass. One of his first activities was to build a fort on the Green River near present-day Pinedale, Wyoming, the site of several fur-trapper rendezvous. Bonneville's military training was evident in his choice of the location for this fort, which was strategically placed and commanded the routes to and from South Pass, Jackson Hole, the Bear River, and Salt Lake. The veteran fur trappers still in the area were not impressed with the fort or Bonneville, however; he was, in their opinion, an interloper, and even worse, a "greenhorn." They called the fort "Bonneville's Folly" and "Fort Nonsense" and predicted that he would have to abandon it.

Their predictions were correct: Beaver was scarce, the established trappers were hostile to Bonneville's men, and the Blackfeet were even more so. In the summer of 1832, Bonneville abandoned the fort and divided his command into two parties. One party went to trap the Bear River. Bonneville, with the remaining men, traveled northwest to Pierre's Hole and then made winter camp on the Salmon River. Throughout these travels, Bonneville was clearly less concerned with collecting beaver pelts and turning a profit than he was with introducing a permanent American presence in territory that had formerly been controlled exclusively by the Hudson's Bay Company.

The following summer, Bonneville decided to retrace the Astorians' route to the junction of the Columbia and Snake rivers, and then to travel to the Bear River and establish a winter camp. He dispatched a separate party as well. The objective of this second group was to locate a route from Great Salt Lake to the Pacific. Bonneville chose a man named Joseph Walker to lead the brigade. Although Walker began his career in the Rockies and the Far West in the waning days of the mountain-man era, he would prove to be as formidable an explorer and frontiersman as any of his storied predecessors, including Jedediah Smith.

Joe Walker's life was the stuff of legends even before he arrived in the Rocky Mountains. He was born Joseph Reddeford Walker in 1799 in the mountains of Tennessee, and he spent his youth moving across the Piedmont Region and Appalachian Mountains with his restless family. He came west in 1818, helped to establish the Santa Fe Trail (and was thrown into prison by the Spanish authorities for his troubles), and fought Indians. In 1827 he was elected sheriff of Independence, Missouri, the kind of riotous boomtown that regularly chewed up sheriffs and spat them out broken men. Not so Walker, who was the kind of lawman who would eventually inspire countless Hollywood westerns. Walker was big, ruggedly handsome, fearless, tough but fair, charismatic, and a deadeye shot, although his reputation was such that he rarely had to draw a gun. After two terms as sheriff he grew restless and in 1832 he signed on with Bonneville's expedition as field commander.

Walker and 40 well-equipped men left the Green River rendezvous site on August 20, 1833, proceeded to Great Salt Lake, and then crossed the desert to the southwest. In eastern Nevada, Walker struck the Humboldt River, a curious stream discovered earlier by Peter Skene Ogden. Walker followed the Humboldt downstream until it disappeared into the swampy, unpleasant Humboldt Sink area at the eastern base of the Sierra Nevada. Here, Walker began to have trouble with the local Digger Indians, and

one morning he and his 40 men found themselves surrounded by about 900 hostiles. The Diggers, however,
were still unfamiliar with the rifle, and Walker's men now
introduced them to this instrument, killing about 40 of
the Indians, who were suitably impressed and let the white
men move on in peace. They continued westward until
their passage was blocked by the imposing Sierra Nevada,
an obstacle that seemed even more daunting than 900
hostile Diggers. It took Walker's party three punishing
weeks to cross the Sierra Nevada, but they were rewarded
as they came down the western side of the range, for they
descended into a place of such beauty and grandeur that
the men were reduced to a state of awestricken silence.
This was the Yosemite Valley, and Walker and his companions were the first white men to look upon its almost
supernatural beauty. Most of them—including Walker—
would remember the descent into the valley as the high
point of their years in the mountains.

As they advanced into California there were more won-
ders. Gigantic redwood forests, a profusion of game and
fish, constant sunshine, a spectacular meteor shower, and
even an earthquake astounded the travelers. They journeyed at their ease all the way to the Pacific at Monterey
Bay, where, unlike Smith, they were cordially received
and entertained by the Spanish authorities (Walker was of
a much more politic nature than Smith, and he succeeded
in charming his hosts whereas Smith only alienated them).
After a good three months of eating and drinking with
various Californians, Walker gathered his men together
and, somewhat reluctantly, they headed back east toward
the wintry mountains.

Back at the base of the Sierra Nevada, Walker hoped
to find an easier route across the range than the one they
had taken on the westward leg of the journey. He found
his passage at the headwaters of the Kern River, and it was
known thereafter as Walker Pass. In the Great Basin again,
the caravan engaged in a march across the Nevada deserts

that was as grueling as any of Smith's desert crossings. Several times the men became so thirsty that they drank the blood of some of the livestock they had brought along for food. Once again they arrived at the Humboldt Sink, once again the Diggers menaced them, and once again the white man's rifles took a heavy toll on the Indians. After that incident it was smooth going, and the expedition arrived at the Bear River rendezvous, where Bonneville awaited them, on July 12, 1834.

Walker's expedition had been wildly successful in all respects. In terms of mountain-man expeditions, the lack of any attrition rate at all was remarkable. Despite the requisite hardships and perils of the frontier, Walker's party suffered not a single casualty (Jed Smith, by comparison, lost 26 men during his California adventures). And in terms of trailblazing and acquisition of important geographic knowledge, Walker's odyssey had crucial results and far-reaching consequences. He and his men had laid out the trail across the Great Basin via the Humboldt River and over the Sierra Nevada via Walker Pass that would eventually be used by thousands of settlers and gold rushers on their way to California. Just as important as these accomplishments were the tales of California brought back across the Rockies by Walker's men. The hardened mountaineers spoke rapturously of a golden land of sunshine, ease, and plenty, and this paradisiacal image of California has persisted down the years and even today continues to lure Americans westward.

The mountain men were encountering a faint, steadily growing trickle of newcomers to the Rockies during the period of Walker's explorations, but unlike Walker, most of these sojourners were greenhorns. Veteran trapper-trader William Sublette, Jed Smith's former business partner, encountered a group of greener-than-usual greenhorns on the lower Missouri in the spring of 1832. They were dressed in outlandish uniforms and were towing ridiculous vehicles—boats with wheels. They called them

(continued on page 108)

The mysterious Captain Benjamin Bonneville arrived in the Rockies in 1832, ostensibly to begin a fur-trade operation. He was most likely engaged in reconnaissance of the Far West for the U.S. government. In a report he wrote for the army, Bonneville advised, "If our Government ever intends taking possession of Oregon, the sooner it shall be done the better."

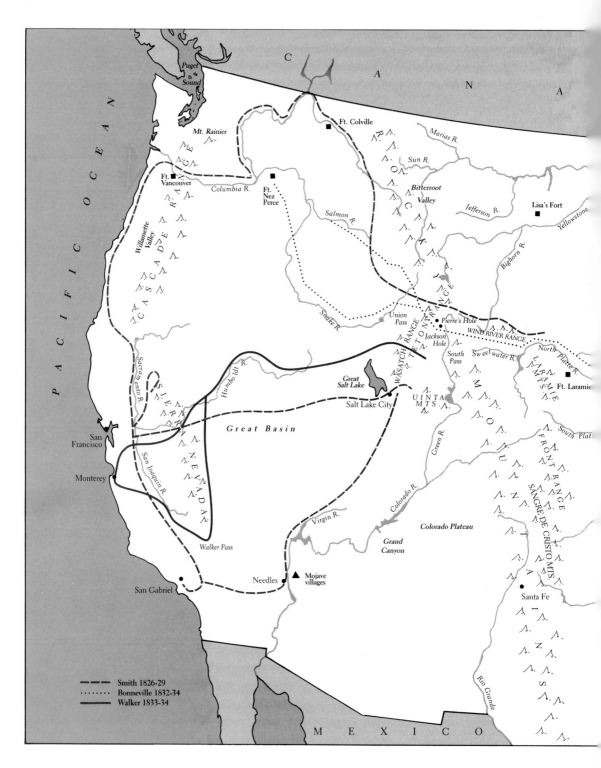

Puget Sound

C A N A D A

PACIFIC OCEAN

Mt. Rainier

Ft. Colville ■

Marias R.

Sun R.

Bitterroot Valley

Jefferson R.

Lisa's Fort ■

Ft. Vancouver ■

Columbia R.

Ft. Nez Perce ■

Salmon R.

Yellowstone

Willamette Valley

Bighorn R.

CASCADE RANGE

Snake R.

Union Pass

Pierre's Hole •

WIND RIVER RANGE

North Platte R.

Sacramento R.

TETON RANGE

Jackson Hole

South Pass

Sweetwater R.

LARAMIE MTS.

Humboldt R.

Great Salt Lake

WASATCH RANGE

Salt Lake City ●

UINTA MTS.

Green R.

Ft. Laramie ■

San Francisco ▼

Great Basin

MONTUN

South Plat

SIERRA NEVADA

Monterey ◀

San Joaquin R.

FRONT RANGE

SANGRE DE CRISTO MTS.

Colorado R.

Virgin R.

Colorado Plateau

Walker Pass

Grand Canyon

San Gabriel ●

Needles ● ▲ *Mojave villages*

Santa Fe ●

Rio Grande

M E X I C O

- - - Smith 1826-29
.... Bonneville 1832-34
——— Walker 1833-34

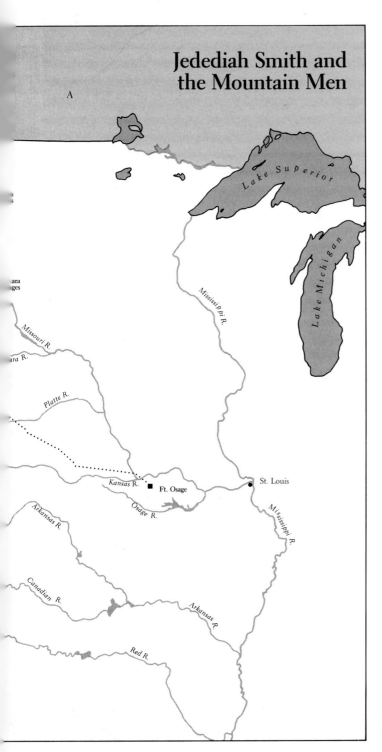

Jedediah Smith and the Mountain Men

A

Lake Superior

Lake Michigan

Mississippi R.

ara
ges

Missouri R.

ra R.

Platte R.

Kansas R. ■ Ft. Osage

● St. Louis

Osage R.

Mississippi R.

Arkansas R.

Canadian R.

Arkansas R.

Red R.

The routes pioneered by Jed Smith, Benjamin Bonneville, and Joseph Walker across the Rockies and the Far West.

Nathaniel Wyeth, an ambitious New England merchant, was perhaps the first American to make a continuous journey from the Atlantic coast to the Pacific coast. Like the waves of easterners who would eventually follow in his footsteps, Wyeth used the trails blazed by the mountain men.

(continued from page 105)

"amphibiums," and hoped the contraptions would make the crossing of the mountains easier. This strange little party was led by a Boston ice merchant, Nathaniel J. Wyeth. Wyeth was the living embodiment of Yankee ingenuity (amphibiums notwithstanding), and the flame of Manifest Destiny burned in his heart as well. As a merchant, Wyeth hoped to turn a profit in the fur trade of the Far West; as an easterner with a patriotic-expansionist bent, he hoped to aid the American cause in Oregon Country and to extend New England culture to the Pacific Northwest.

Bill Sublette took pity on Wyeth's little band of would-be mountaineers, told them to get rid of the amphibiums, and offered to guide them at least part of the way across the Rockies. Sublette was bound for the summer rendezvous at Pierre's Hole, and Wyeth and his tenderfoot New Englanders gratefully followed him into the Rockies and across South Pass to the rendezvous site, undergoing a crash course in mountain-man skills in the process. They arrived at Pierre's Hole in time to meet some of the greatest mountain men yet living and to assist them in a pitched battle with a war party of Gros Ventre Indians. Wyeth fought well and won his first measure of respect from the mountain men.

In August 1832, Wyeth headed west from Pierre's Hole, then north, cutting across the Snake River plain. In October he crossed the Blue Mountains to the junction of the Snake and Columbia and traveled down the Columbia to Fort Vancouver. Before he had left Boston, Wyeth had taken a page from John Jacob Astor's book and dispatched a ship to meet him at the mouth of the Columbia. But, like Astor's *Tonquin*, Wyeth's ship met with disaster; it never reached the Columbia, having gone down at sea, and Wyeth's enterprise went down with it. The Yankee spent the winter of 1832–33 in the company of Hudson's Bay men at Fort Vancouver, watching that operation closely and learning the ins and outs of the fur trade from those who were best at it. The following summer saw him at the Hudson's Bay Flathead Post in western Montana; he traveled south from this point to the Tetons, where he met with Bonneville. The two men made plans for a trip to California (the trip that Walker would take later that summer), but Wyeth backed out of the project and headed home for New England.

Wyeth's first western venture may have been an economic disaster, but in terms of knowledge and experience gained it had been lucrative, and when the Bostonian launched his second trip west in the summer of 1834 he could no longer be considered a greenhorn. During the winter he had planned an elaborate scheme: He would send a ship to the mouth of the Columbia to trade in furs and pick up a load of salmon. Wyeth, meanwhile, would go to the summer rendezvous with trade goods, exchange them for beaver pelts, and head northwest for the Columbia and the waiting vessel that would carry the wealth in fur and pickled salmon back to New England. Accompanying Wyeth west would be two scientists and two missionaries. One historian has noted that the primary importance of Wyeth's second expedition "was that it opened up the Oregon Trail and the Northwest to the two chief forces of contemporary civilization, science and organized Protestant Christianity."

In terms of the routes followed, Wyeth's second western expedition was almost a duplicate of his first. The second expedition also duplicated the earlier venture in terms of economic success, or the lack of it. When Wyeth reached the rendezvous, he discovered that the trappers were now hostile toward him; competition for the remaining fur resources in the West had given rise to a cutthroat atmosphere among the trappers, who refused to deal with the Yankee interloper. And when he reached the mouth of the Columbia he learned that for the second year in a row the ship that was supposed to meet him there had been lost at sea. By the spring of 1836, Wyeth's second venture was over and he left the West to other men.

Although Wyeth himself might have considered his western enterprise a personal failure, in terms of the westward expansion of the United States it was a great success. On his way north to the Columbia in 1835, he had built Fort Hall, near the junction of the Snake and Portneuf rivers. This fort gave the United States a solid foothold in that territory as well as a strong arguing point in the debate with Great Britain over eventual control of the Pacific Northwest. It also, in later years, served as a critical point on the Oregon Trail. On Wyeth's return trip in 1836 he mapped the Willamette Valley and proved conclusively that the Multnomah River of Lewis and Clark was, like the Buenaventura, a river of the imagination. Upon his return to Boston, Wyeth spread word of the Oregon Trail to his fellow New Englanders, who would make frequent use of the trail in the coming years. And when he quit the Oregon territory in 1836 he left behind the two New England missionaries, Jason and Daniel Lee, who formed the nucleus of the first permanent American settlement in that region.

With each passing year, the geographic knowledge of the fur trappers and traders was put to practical use by a growing stream of westering Americans. In 1841, guided by the heroic mountain man Thomas Fitzpatrick and following the Humboldt River route pioneered by Thomas Walker, an Illinois schoolteacher named John Bidwell led a wagon train to California. The Bidwell party crossed the Plains via the Platte River, traversed South Pass, and then pushed on to the Bear River. From the Bear they veered south to the Humboldt and traveled west through its valley to the foot of the Sierra Nevada. They crossed the mountains over Sonora Pass, discovered by Walker, and traveled down the Stanislaus River, where Jed Smith's men had wintered, to the Sacramento Valley. The Lees in Oregon and the Bidwell party in California were the forerunners of a huge migration to follow between 1842 and the Civil War, and neither these forerunners nor those who followed them could have made the transcontinental crossing without the geographic information provided by the mountain men.

The last great rendezvous of the fur trappers was held in the summer of 1838. Although the rendezvous was as riotous as usual, it was also pervaded by a melancholy atmosphere, for the fur-trade days were almost over, and the trappers sensed the passing of an era. Many of the trappers who had survived those wild years would soon vanish into obscurity, but many were to continue to be an important feature of the American West. Their future role was typified by Thomas Fitzpatrick's service as guide to the Bidwell party; mountain men would continue to guide emigrants across the plains, the Rockies, and the Great Basin. Some, like Jim Bridger, would establish posts and forts along the emigrant trails where supplies could be replenished. Others, such as Kit Carson, would serve as guides for the wave of government explorers who began an official reconnaissance of the West in the 1840s.

Consider what the mountain men had accomplished in the years between John Colter in 1806 and Joseph Walker in 1835. They had demolished myths and misconceptions and replaced them with solid geographic realities. William Clark's distorted view of a common source region and Thomas Jefferson's dream of a water passage across the continent had been replaced by the realities of the Oregon Trail and South Pass. The mythical Buenaventura had finally begun to vanish from maps, to be replaced by the Humboldt River and the Walker and Sonora passes across the Sierra Nevada. And no longer was the West viewed as a uniform garden; the practitioners of the fur trade had discovered that much of it was desert, particularly the lands west of the Rockies. But they had also learned that the Far West—especially Oregon Country and the Great Valley of California—did indeed contain the prime agricultural land that might host an expanding America.

Frontier schoolteacher John Bidwell was part of the first overland immigrant train to cross the Rockies and reach California. They set out in May 1841 and reached their destination in November. Their guide was the renowned mountain man Thomas Fitzpatrick.

The mountain men's greatest legacy—the Oregon Trail.

The toils of the mountain men had effected a fundamental change in the American people's perception of the Far West. No longer was it a land of myth and mystery; no longer was it considered to be the Great Unknown. The mountain men had, in effect, helped to annex the West by making it familiar to the common American; a more formal annexation was not far behind, for once Americans began to view the West as a geographic extension of their already settled lands and as such, a place that could be reached, a place that could be gotten to, it was not long before they made it so practically and politically. In this way, men such as John Colter and George Drouillard, Wilson Price Hunt and Robert Stuart, Jim Bridger and Edward Rose, Andrew Henry and William Ashley, Jedediah Smith and Joseph Walker, and all the other members of that rugged breed, known and unknown, made a crucial contribution to America's development into a continental nation.

Further Reading

Alter, J. Cecil. *James Bridger: Trapper, Frontiersman, Scout, and Guide*. Salt Lake City: Shepherd, 1925.

Bieber, Ralph, ed. *Exploring Southwestern Trails: 1846–1854*. Glendale, CA: Clark, 1977.

Burdett, Charles. *The Life and Adventures of Kit Carson*. New York: Dwight Evans, 1860.

Carter, H. L. *Dear Old Kit*. Norman: University of Oklahoma Press, 1968.

Cline, Gloria Griffen. *Exploring the Great Basin*. Norman: University of Oklahoma Press, 1963.

Clokey, Richard M. *William H. Ashley: Enterprise and Politics in the Trans-Mississippi West*. Norman: University of Oklahoma Press, 1980.

Dale, Harrison Clifford. *The Ashley-Smith Explorations and the Discovery of a Central Route to the Pacific, 1822–1829*. Rev. ed. Glendale, CA: Clark, 1941.

De Voto, Bernard. *Across the Wide Missouri*. Boston: Houghton Mifflin, 1947.

———. *The Course of Empire*. Boston: Houghton Mifflin, 1952.

———. *The Year of Decision*. Boston: Houghton Mifflin, 1942.

Favour, Alpheus. *Old Bill Williams: Mountain Man*. Chapel Hill: University of North Carolina Press, 1936.

Flores, Dan L. *Jefferson and Southwest Exploration*. Norman: University of Oklahoma Press, 1984.

Fulton, Maurice G., ed. *The Diary and Letters of Josiah Gregg*. 2 vols. Norman: University of Oklahoma Press, 1941–44.

Goetzmann, William H. *Army Exploration in the American West, 1803–1863*. New Haven: Yale University Press, 1959.

———. *Exploration and Empire: The Explorer and the Scientist in the Winning of the American West*. New York: Knopf, 1966.

Harris, Burton. *John Colter: His Years in the Rocky Mountains*. Casper, WY: Big Horn, 1983.

Hawgood, John A. *America's Western Frontiers*. New York: Knopf, 1967.

Hollon, W. Eugene. *The Great American Desert: Then and Now*. New York: Oxford University Press, 1966.

Jackson, Donald, ed. *The Journals of Zebulon Montgomery Pike*. 2 vols. Norman: University of Oklahoma Press, 1966.

———. *Thomas Jefferson and the Stony Mountains: Exploring the West from Monticello*. Urbana: University of Illinois Press, 1981.

Merk, Merrill J. *History of the Westward Movement*. New York: Knopf, 1978.

———. *The Oregon Question*. Cambridge, MA: Belknap Press, 1967.

Morgan, Dale L. *Jedediah Smith and the Opening of the West*. Lincoln: University of Nebraska Press, 1964.

Sandoz, Mari. *The Beaver Men*. Lincoln: University of Nebraska Press, 1978.

Skarsten, M. O. *George Drouillard: Hunter and Interpreter*. Glendale, CA: Clark, 1964.

Smith, Henry Nash. *Virgin Land: The American West in Symbol and Myth*. New York: Vintage Books, 1950.

Sprague, Marshall. *The Great Gates: The Story of the Rocky Mountain Passes*. Boston: Little, Brown, 1964.

Chronology

Entries in roman type refer directly to the mountain men, the fur trade, and the exploration of the American West; entries in italics refer to related historical events.

1793	*Fur trader Alexander Mackenzie reaches the Pacific Ocean after traversing overland from Lake Athabasca*
1801	*Thomas Jefferson elected president of the United States*
1803	*United States buys the Louisiana Territory from France; Jefferson charges Meriwether Lewis and William Clark to undertake a "voyage of discovery" to explore the Missouri River in search of a route to the Pacific*
1804–06	*Lewis and Clark expedition reaches the Pacific Ocean, opening new territory for westward expansion*
1807	Manuel Lisa organizes his first fur-trapping venture and constructs Fort Raymond on the Yellowstone River; hires John Colter, a veteran of the Lewis and Clark expedition; Colter and George Drouillard explore the Bighorn Basin, Absaroka Mountains, and the Wind River valley
1809–11	Drouillard killed in attack by Blackfeet on the Missouri; Colter retires soon afterward; Andrew Henry crosses the Continental Divide and builds the first American trading post west of the Rocky Mountains; Fort Astoria, financed by John Jacob Astor, constructed on the Columbia River
1812	Robert Stuart discovers the South Pass through the Rocky Mountains, opening what will become the Oregon Trail
1813	Fort Astoria sold to the North West Company for $40,000; Astorians and Northwesters throw a wild party to celebrate the sale
1816–19	Donald McKenzie explores the area between the western Rockies and the eastern Cascades
1821–23	Using McKenzie's methods, the Taos trappers prosper, helping develop the St. Louis–Santa Fe trade route

1824	Free trappers emerge in the Northwest; Jedediah Smith and John Weber explore the area from Powder River to Wind River valley; Smith crosses South Pass
1826–28	Smith discovers the southern route to California, crosses the Great Basin and the Sierra Nevadas, explores the Great Valley of California and southern Oregon
1830	Explores the Bighorn and Judith River basins; returns to St. Louis
1831	While on a trip to Santa Fe, Smith is attacked and killed by a band of Comanche Indians
1832–35	Benjamin Bonneville and Nathaniel Wyeth explore the area west of South Pass and the Oregon Trail; Joseph Walker discovers the Humboldt River and the California Trail from the Great Salt Lake to the Sacramento Valley; Wyeth builds Fort Hall, the first permanent American establishment west of the Continental Divide
1838	Last fur-trade rendezvous is held on the Green River in west-central Wyoming

Index

Picture Credits

From *Astoria*, Rare Book and Manuscript Division, The New York Public Library, Astor, Lenox and Tilden Foundations: p. 59; Courtesy the Bancroft Library: p. 83; Karl Bodmer, State Historical Society of North Dakota: pp. 27 *Grizzly Bear*, 31 *Bull Boats, Mandan Village*, 45 *Keel Boat near Piegan Camp*, 74 *Arikara Warrior*, 85 *Crow Indians*; Caleb Boyle, *Thomas Jefferson at the National Bridge*, Kirby Collection of Historical Paintings, Lafayette College, Easton, PA: p. 21; California State Library: pp. 86, 94, 111, 112; George Catlin, *St. Louis from the River Below*, National Museum of American Art, Washington, DC/Art Resource, NY: p. 15; Colorado Historical Society: p. 88; Stanley Del, State Historical Society of North Dakota: p. 26; Gabriel Franchere, Library of Congress, from *Narrative of a Voyage to the Northwest Coast of America in the Years 1811, 1812, 1813, and 1814*: pp. 42, 44; Hudson's Bay Company Archives, Provincial Archives of Manitoba: pp. 64, 97; Washington Irving, from *The Adventures of Capt. Bonneville*, vol. 1, Rare Book and Manuscript Division, The New York Public Library, Astor, Lenox and Tilden Foundations: p. 33; Vikki Leib (map): pp. 106–7; From *Life in California, 1846*, Library of Congress: p. 92; Alfred Jacob Miller, *Buffalo Hunt*, the Philbrook Museum of Art, Tulsa, OK: pp. 50–51; Alfred Jacob Miller, *Crow Chief on the Lookout*, the Rockwell Museum, Corning, NY: p. 50; Alfred Jacob Miller, *The Halt*, Sheldon Memorial Art Gallery, University of Nebraska, Lincoln: p. 55; Alfred Jacob Miller, *Pipe of Peace at the Rendezvous*, Stark Museum of Art, Orange, TX: pp. 52–53; Alfred Jacob Miller, *Portrait of Captain Joseph Reddeford Walker*, Joslyn Art Museum, Omaha, NE: p. 100; Alfred Jacob Miller, Walters Art Gallery, Baltimore, MD: pp. 46 *Wind River Chain*, 49 *Portrait of Antoine* (detail), 54 *Jim Bridger in Armor at the Green River Rendezvous*, 56 *Storm-waiting for the Caravan*; Courtesy of the Missouri Historical Society: pp. 12, 14, 17, 18, 28, 35, 36, 40, 47, 78, 80, 82, 90, 91, 96, 105; Montana Historical Society, Helena: p. 62; National Archives of Canada: p. 60 (neg. #C82974); Charles Willson Peale, State Historical Society of North Dakota: pp. 22 *Meriwether Lewis*, 23 *William Clark*; C. M. Russell, *Free Trappers*, Mackey Collection, Montana Historical Society: p. 102; O. C. Seltzer, *Manuel Lisa Watching the Construction of Fort Lisa*, the Thomas Gilcrease Institute of American History and Art, Tulsa, OK: p. 32; Utah State Historical Society: pp. 57, 69; Washington State Historical Society, Tacoma: p. 108; From *Wilderness Kingdom: Indian Life in the Rocky Mountains 1840–1847; the Journals and Paintings of Nicholas Point, S. J.*, published by Loyola University Press, 1967. Reprinted with permission of the publisher: p. 65; Courtesy of Frank Wolfskill: p. 66

John Logan Allen is a professor of geography at the University of Connecticut. He received bachelor's and master's degrees from the University of Wyoming and a doctorate from Clark University. He has written extensively about geography and exploration and is the author of *Passage Through the Garden: Lewis and Clark and the Image of the American Northwest*.

William H. Goetzmann holds the Jack S. Blanton, Sr., Chair in History at the University of Texas at Austin, where he has taught for many years. The author of numerous works on American history and exploration, he won the 1967 Pulitzer and Parkman prizes for his *Exploration and Empire: The Role of the Explorer and Scientist in the Winning of the American West, 1800–1900*. With his son William N. Goetzmann, he coauthored *The West of the Imagination*, which received the Carr P. Collins Award in 1986 from the Texas Institute of Letters. His documentary television series of the same name received a blue ribbon in the history category at the American Film and Video Festival held in New York City in 1987. A recent work, *New Lands, New Men: America and the Second Great Age of Discovery*, was published in 1986 to much critical acclaim.

Michael Collins served as command module pilot on the *Apollo 11* space mission, which landed his colleagues Neil Armstrong and Buzz Aldrin on the moon. A graduate of the United States Military Academy, Collins was named an astronaut in 1963. In 1966 he piloted the *Gemini 10* mission, during which he became the third American to walk in space. The author of several books on space exploration, Collins was director of the Smithsonian Institution's National Air and Space Museum from 1971 to 1978 and is a recipient of the Presidential Medal of Freedom.